Cities in the
Technology Economy

**MAXINE GOODMAN LEVIN
COLLEGE OF URBAN AFFAIRS**

Cleveland State University

Cities and Contemporary Society

Series Editors: Richard D. Bingham and Larry C. Ledebur,
Cleveland State University

Sponsored by the
Maxine Goodman Levin College of Urban Affairs
Cleveland State University

This new series focuses on key topics and emerging trends in urban
policy. Each volume is specially prepared for academic use, as well as
for specialists in the field.

SUBURBAN SPRAWL
Private Decisions and Public Policy
Wim Wiewel and Joseph J. Persky, Editors

THE INFRASTRUCTURE OF PLAY
Building the Tourist City
Dennis R. Judd, Editor

THE ADAPTED CITY
Institutional Dynamics and Structural Change
H. George Frederickson, Gary A. Johnson, and Curtis H. Wood

CREDIT TO THE COMMUNITY
Community Reinvestment and Fair Lending Policy
in the United States
Dan Immergluck

PARTNERSHIPS FOR SMART GROWTH
University-Community Collaboration for Better Public Places
Wim Wiewel and Gerrit-Jan Knaap, Editors

REVITALIZING THE CITY
Strategies to Contain Sprawl and Revive the Core
*Fritz W. Wagner, Timothy E. Joder, Anthony J. Mumphrey, Jr.,
Krishna M. Akundi, and Alan F.J. Artibise*

THE UNIVERSITY AS URBAN DEVELOPER
Case Studies and Analysis
David C. Perry and Wim Wiewel, Editors

PEOPLE AND THE COMPETITIVE ADVANTAGE OF PLACE
Building a Workforce for the 21st Century
Shari Garmise

CITIES IN THE TECHNOLOGY ECONOMY
Darrene L. Hackler

Cities in the
Technology Economy

Darrene L. Hackler

CITIES AND
CONTEMPORARY
SOCIETY

M.E.Sharpe
Armonk, New York
London, England

Library of Congress Cataloging-in-Publication Data

Hackler, Darrene L., 1970–
Cities in the technology economy / by Darrene L. Hackler.
  p. cm. — (Cities and contemporary society)
Includes bibliographical references and index.
ISBN 13: 978-0-7656-1269-4 (cloth : alk. paper)
ISBN 10: 0-7656-1269-0 (cloth : alk. paper)
1. City planning. 2. Cities and towns—Effect of technological innovations on.
3. Technology—Economic aspects. 4. Technology—Social aspects. I. Title. II. Series.

HT166.H335 2006
307.76—dc22   2006005851

Printed in the United States of America

The paper used in this publication meets the minimum requirements of
American National Standard for Information Sciences
Permanence of Paper for Printed Library Materials,
ANSI Z 39.48-1984.

BM (c)   10   9   8   7   6   5   4   3   2   1

To Chris, you are an inspiration and a true companion;
To my family, for their unconditional love and support.

Contents

List of Tables

Preface

The seeds of this research were planted in the mid-to-late 1990s, while I was completing my graduate research and working for a think tank at the Claremont Graduate University in Claremont, California. Several phenomena conspired to steer me in directions that ultimately led to this book. First, I was, as all somewhat idealistic graduate students, seeking an emerging field of work—particularly one that bridged my interdisciplinary interests in the fields of public policy, economics, and political science. Second, it was a time of unprecedented technological and economic growth, fueling popular interest in and analysis of the effects of technology on all aspects of public and private life. Third, for whatever reasons, it became "cool" to study cities again, and particularly exciting for a small-town kid from Idaho. Living in the metropolitan laboratory of Los Angeles during this period certainly provided an intellectually stimulating backdrop for the confluence of these phenomena and my examination of the relationships among technology, cities, and economic development.

Much of my interest in understanding the impact of technology on cities and local governments is traceable back to my work with Thomas Horan at the Claremont Graduate University. The research we conducted for the Lincoln Institute of Land Policy with Benjamin Chinitz on the information revolution and its unfolding effects on human settlement and business location patterns provided intellectual fodder (Chinitz, Horan, and Hackler 1996). What the popular press billed as titanic sea changes had yet to be connected to the operations and activities of local governments—cities, towns, and counties, and their surrounding regions. Technology's unique effect on daily life and operations appeared to be overarching and to be fundamentally changing many of the ways in which people live, work, and relate to institutions. Isolating what was meant by technology and how it affects local governments' abilities to provide economic opportunities and livable communities was a large challenge.

The research presented in this book is positioned in a field of study that is rapidly developing from a theoretical and empirical standpoint and is of pivotal importance to policymakers seeking to understand the nexus between technological and economic changes and institutions. The technology economy presents many challenges to cities and local governments. Recognizing the pivotal role that local governments play in the technology economy, this book examines the effect of technology industries and infrastructure on cities and the local policy actions to respond to these changes.

In seeking to test existing frameworks and develop new frameworks for application and testing, I am seeking, as many others are, to better inform this field of study. Many friends, colleagues, and advisors were vital to this work. I especially appreciate the discussions with and comments from Annette Steinacker, Michael Pagano, Susan Clarke, Gary Gaile, Dennis Judd, Bill Barnes, Priscilla Regan, Julianne Mahler, and Kara Serrano. I value the assistance of Joe Rude, a graduate student who is every professor's dream—inquisitive, helpful, thorough, and enthusiastic. I value as well the willingness of students Erik Porse, Doug Scott, Lynn Chapman, and Elizabeth Wheel to engage in serious research in a course on how cities are using forms of technology as assets. I thank Dick Bingham, series editor, and Harry Briggs at M.E. Sharpe for providing motivation, enthusiasm, and guidance through the publishing process. Finally, the intellectual and spiritual support of Christopher Hoene, to whom I am eternally grateful, enabled the development of these ideas and provided critical feedback during a stressful period of time.

I am grateful for research support from the College of Arts and Sciences at George Mason University through its Junior Faculty Award in the Social Sciences and Sciences. I am also grateful to the National League of Cities, which provided access to its membership, and interaction with and feedback from city officials engaged in the question of how technology is shaping the future of their cities. Discussions with the following individuals highlighted real concerns, kept my work grounded, and provided ongoing reinforcement for the importance of this research: Mark Linder, assistant city manager of San Jose, California; Jim Dailey, mayor of Little Rock, Arkansas; Brenda Barger, former mayor of Watertown, South Dakota; Steve Burkholder, mayor of Lakewood, Colorado; Ron Bates, former city council member of Los Alamitos, California; and Margaret Peterson, city council member of West Valley City, Utah. Finally, my research benefited from the willingness of the following city officials to share their views and information, from the economic development officials responding to surveys to individual staff providing interviews: Linda Poissant of Charlotte, North Carolina; Richard Mulligan and Corey Gherkin of Mesa, Arizona; Rashid Ahmed of Portland, Oregon; Patricia Cook of Lansing, Michigan; Kimberly Walesh, Timm Borden, and Richard Bertalan of San Jose, California; Zach Montgomery of Roswell, New Mexico; Chris Dalton of Long Beach, California; Paul Morris and Roger Black, Utah Open Infrastructure Agency; and Geoffrey Lewis of Boston, Massachusetts. All errors and omissions are my own.

Cities in the
Technology Economy

MAXINE GOODMAN LEVIN
COLLEGE OF URBAN AFFAIRS

Cleveland State University

The Dawn of the Technology Economy

The broad outlines of our electronically mediated future—if not the details—are becoming clear. One way or another, depending on the outcomes of the technology races, business battles, and public policy debates of the millennium's end, these disparate ingredients will eventually combine to produce a worldwide digital information infrastructure. The potential benefits of this are so great, and the momentum for it is building so rapidly, that nothing will effectively stand in the way. . . . It will increasingly become the key to opportunity and development, and the enabler of new social constructions and urban patterns.

—*William J. Mitchell*

[E]conomic development policies at the state and local level have become preoccupied with fashioning strategies that would attract, retain, and "home grow" high tech industries and firms.

—*Karen Chapple, Ann Markusen, Greg Schrock,*
Daisaku Yamamoto, and Pingkang Yu

During the 1990s, observers of economic, social, and technological change began to perceive that the world was changing in increasingly rapid and intense ways. We witnessed the emergence of the home computer as a device used for something beyond video games; the first Internet web browser and e-mail accounts; a need for multiple phone lines for Internet access and fax machines; a growing array of miniature electronic devices enabling constant communication—pagers, cell phones, personal digital assistants, and BlackBerries; and increasing opportunities to purchase items and pay bills online. We also witnessed a burgeoning government presence online, from e-government's delivered information and services to e-democracy's promise of new forms of civic engagement. New industries emerged, like Internet and application service providers, developing because of the pervasive use of and reliance on technology and furthering usage and reliance upon technology through the generation of new services and products. Telecommunications, technology, information, and Internet companies sprouted and grew like weeds, growing at an unprecedented pace economically and passing business plans around venture capital funds like cards around a poker table. Public offerings of these companies made instant millionaires out of software programmers and other techno-geeks. Painted orange-and-white lines began to appear regularly on city streets, mapping routes with techno-babble directions and signs of where companies could tear up streets to lay fiber-optic cable. Amid these changes, and in many respects driven by these changes, the U.S. economy rode the largest bull market in U.S. history.

All segments of society have a personal narrative describing these trends, whether an individual, private business, nonprofit organization, or government, and the struggle to name these sets of trends continues. Although some seek to define them economically—"new economy" (Progressive Policy Institute 2000; Kelly 1998; Hilton 2001; Rondinelli 2001; Salvesen and Renski 2002; Atkinson and Gottlieb 2001; Sommers and Carlson 2000; Bresnahan and Gambardella 2004), "high-tech economy" (DeVol 1999; Markusen, Hall, and Glasmeier 1986; Chapple et al. 2004; Scott 1993; Pollard and Storper 1996), and "digital economy" (Brynjolfsson and Kahin 2000; Tapscott 1996)—others associate broader trends or impacts on geography, like the "death of distance" (Cairncross 1995), the "technological reshaping of metropolian America" (U.S. Department of Commerce, Office of Technology Assessment 1995), geographies of the digital or telecommunications revolution (Kotkin 2000; Audretsch and Feldman 2000), and the regional economy (Barnes and Ledebur 1998; Porter 1998; Saxenian 1996; Storper 1995; Scott 1993). Some look at the change through the lens of urban planning or architecture (Graham 1999; Mitchell 1996; Horan 2000). Still others are relating these changes to occupation-defining class structures, like Richard Florida's research on the "creative class" (Florida 2002, 2005a, 2005b) or Robert Reich's "symbolic analysts" (Reich 1991). Regardless of the label, the 1990s witnessed a perfect storm of technological and economic change, and although it didn't quite fit futurists' Blade Runneresque or *Neuromancer* (Gibson 1984) predictions, the changes have had, and continue to have, broad ramifications economically, socially, and politically. The bursting of the United States' technologically driven economic bubble in 2001 has provided an opportunity both to reflect upon the ramifications of the changes that occurred in the 1990s and to take a more reasoned look at where these trends are headed. One thing is clear—the bubble may have burst, but the relationship between economic growth and technological innovation remains strong.

The Technology Economy

Common mistakes made in examining technology's impacts on the economy, governments, or other institutions involve taking too broad or too narrow a view, and exaggerating or underestimating technology's influence. Just as the vignettes offered above can be construed to be a result of multiple factors beyond technology, too much refinement in determining technology's impact can lead to myopic conclusions. Analyses of technology have often focused on technology as an economic sector or as an infrastructure needing investment. This book strives to be grounded in both worlds, attempting to analyze technology's role in the economy, as well as assessing the capacity and issues surrounding technology infrastructure, with a particular focus on local areas and the activities of local governments. I describe two related phenomena, technology-driven economic change and the development of local technology infrastructure that accompanies this change—the combination of which I refer to as the *technology economy*. The goal of this book is to define the technology economy as it concerns cities.

Technology and Economic Change

The wedding of technology and economic change is not new. Technological change has always been one factor that economists recognize as expanding production possibility frontiers—producing more with the same level of inputs. However, the sheer impact of technology on the economy, given recent experiences, is worthy of more attention. During the latter part of the 1990s, information technology–producing industries accounted for nearly one-third of U.S. domestic economic growth, and employment increased 51.9 percent, from 3.5 to 5.4 million jobs, between 1993 and 2000 (U.S. Department of Commerce 2003, Economic Statistics Administration).[1] The zeal attached to these industries fueled much of the stock market's climb over this period. As we now know, the success of these industries did not insulate them from macroeconomic trends and an eight-month-long recession in 2001. In fact, just as technology industries fueled the growth in the 1990s, their decline may have contributed substantially to the downturn in 2001 and its fallout. From 2001 to 2002, employment in information technology–producing industries declined 10.7 percent, with manufacturing employment in these industries declining 15.8 percent and services employment in these industries declining by 8.8 percent. Other private industries experienced job losses of only 1.6 percent between 2001 and 2002. A similar trend is born out in the high-technology industries with greater-than-average intensity in science and technology occupations. Employment in these industries increased 12.7 percent between 1992 and 2002, but decreased by 6.2 percent between 2002 and 2004.[2] Despite the downturn, there are signs of resiliency returning across these industries. As of the end of 2004, the real value added for information technology–producing industries increased 14.7 percent. These industries accounted for just 4.2 percent of U.S. current-dollar gross domestic product (GDP), but contributed 0.58 percent to real GDP growth, which is about the same as the entire goods-producing sector (Strassner and Howells 2005).[3]

Technology's impact on the economy goes beyond current conditions to concerns about future economic prosperity. Through the application of new technologies and the associated innovation that continues to transform devices, additional applications, standards, and practices, the economy generates greater competitive advantages. Technology's capacity to encourage and accelerate innovation is its true strength (Audretsch and Feldman 2000). Former Secretary of Labor Robert Reich recently claimed that concerns with technology job losses from the 2001 economic recession and subsequent outsourcing are somewhat unfounded because the United States' competitive advantage is not about keeping jobs associated with mature product cycles; instead, it is about the employees and jobs that are more innovative, ones that provide higher value-added functions, such as invention, creation, integration, key research and development, and basic architecture (Reich 2003).

> [E]ven as the supply of workers around the world capable of high-tech innovation increases, the demand for innovative people is increasing at an even faster pace. . . . [T]he long-term trend is toward greater rewards to people who are at or near the frontiers of information technology—as well as biotechnology, nanotechnology and new-materials technologies. Bigger pay packages are also in store for the professionals (lawyers, bank-

ers, venture capitalists, advertisers, marketers and managers) who cluster around high-tech workers and who support innovative enterprises. (Reich 2003, B3)

Similarly, Florida argues that greater concern should be focused on recent losses in U.S. innovative capacity, as opposed to the loss of less innovative jobs in technology and other industries (Florida 2002). Drawing on these arguments, the technology economy that I describe in this book is not limited to a definition of a sector of the economy. The technology economy encompasses a powerful set of sectors and industries in the economy, generates competitive advantage across industries, operates in an economy increasingly defined by regional competition and globalization, and provides a foundation for future, longer-term economic growth and innovation.

Technology Infrastructure

The technology economy is not just the economic sectors and growth generated across these sectors. It also refers to and includes the actual technologies that enable innovation—the technology infrastructure, comprised primarily of information technology and telecommunications. Computers and their networks, networking hardware, software applications, and the telecommunications networks that allow the flow of communications across these platforms are the infrastructures that facilitate technology's presence in the economy. The Internet is a prime example; as the world's largest computer network, its usage has grown 146.2 percent from 2000 to 2005 (www.InternetWorldStats.com 2005), and the broadband technologies providing faster access to the Internet than the standard modem are disseminating opportunities to a wider audience. A recent report suggests that the rollout of broadband services to 50 percent of U.S. homes (currently only available in approximately 20 percent of homes) would add $140 billion to U.S. GDP as a result of increased service subscriptions, sales of technology equipment, cost reductions from increased telecommuting, and the expansion of e-commerce, new entertainment applications, and healthcare services (Randall, Jackson, and Singer 2003). Yet the United States is lagging in this broadband competition, currently sixteenth in the global rankings of broadband penetration, which is way behind the leading countries of South Korea, Hong Kong, and the Netherlands (International Telecommunication

Union 2005a). This is a concern for the United States' economic future because technology, in useful forms like the Internet, permeates the day-to-day lives of us all, whether man, woman, organization, or machine. Business operations are absorbing technology with the promise of increased efficiencies that allow for redesigned processes like just-in-time manufacturing, distribution, and processing. "Information technology dramatically increases the amount and timeliness of information available to economic agents—and the productivity of processes to organize, process, communicate, store, and retrieve information . . . [thereby impacting] countries, as producers and users of this technology" (Hanna 1994, 1). Governments are finding ways to incorporate technology into their service delivery mechanisms as citizens' expectations rise and they call for faster service that is only a click away. The result is e-government, which includes development of websites and portals to bring citizen services online and bring about the integration of agency processes. The business of e-government is large, with state and local governments spending $700 million in 2002 before the recession contracted most budgets, and a recent series of reports on federal government spending indicate e-government solutions in 2004 accounted for $4 billion (Input 2004a, 2004b, 2005).

Reliance on technological improvements improves people's quality of life at some level—providing access to needed information about jobs and educational opportunities, easier access to family and friends not living in close proximity to one another, and various forms of entertainment. However, the bigger picture of technology infrastructure's relationship to the economy has even greater long-term implications. Dennis Rondinelli suggests that competitiveness in today's economy is reliant upon the creation of information and telecommunication networks (Rondinelli 2001), and several studies demonstrate increases in employment, positive spillover effects on other industries, and increases in regional output all because of technology infrastructure investment. At the state level, research has shown that telecommunications investment is complementary to other physical infrastructure investment (roads and utilities), and often leads to increases in average annual pay, per capita income, and education levels (Dholakia and Harlem 1994). In addition, a state's telecommunications capital stock and industries' utilization of that stock produce differential effects on industry output. For example, service sector output is larger because of greater efficiency in utilization of telecommunications in states with better telecommunications stock (Yilmaz and Dinc 2002). The research stresses that it is important for state and local government to understand each sector's relative demand for telecommunications because overinvestment in telecommunications in localities where industrial sectors do not have great demands for it can result in noneffective uses of public monies. Regardless, a locality's access to advanced products and services influences investment patterns, firm location, and employment growth (Atkinson and Gottlieb 2001).

The Technology Economy and Cities

In this book I seek to define the technology economy as it specifically relates to cities and city governments. Although a national or global perspective might be considered equally appropriate, it is at the local level that the effects of the technology economy are likely to have the most variance. At the local level, the influences of geography, demographics, and political and economic structures create a range of possible technology economy interactions. Understanding the factors contributing to local variance is therefore necessary to understanding national and global trends.

Examining the technology economy in cities stresses the significance of geography to this relationship. "Place is the key economic and social organizing unit of our time. It is place that solves the chicken-and-egg problem, matching people to jobs, jobs to people. . . . Places provide the ecosystems that harness human creativity and turn it into economic value" (Florida 2002, xix). In recognizing geography's potential effect, most explorations of economic growth select regions as the most suitable geographical unit with which to analyze economic relationships (Markusen, Hall, and Glasmeier 1986; Kotkin 2000; Barnes and Ledebur 1998; Florida 2002; Saxenian 1996; Bresnahan and Gambardella 2004; Storper 1995; Atkinson and Gottlieb 2001). There are two consequential differences between those studies and this study of the technology economy. First, most studies focus on an economic or occupational sector as it is related to economic growth. In contrast, my definition of the technology economy recognizes the interrelationships of economic sectors and technology infrastructure as consequential to future long-term growth and development. How the infrastructure supplies both innovative capacity and a supporting foundation is integral to the technology economy's effects. Second, regions, no matter how well they represent a natural segment of the national economy, lack operational governments and subsequent policymaking institutions. It is widely believed that technology infrastructure and well-designed public policies play a critical role in economic growth of a region. How policies influence factors such as availability of skilled technical labor, managerial occupations, and access to capital (venture capital funds), while serving to create an entrepreneurial environment that includes both external and internal information sharing, can ultimately decide the success of a location and its economic prosperity (Bresnahan, Gamardella, and Saxenian 2001). When examining how an area develops an advantage in the technology economy, it is clear that the area of interest must have the capacity to design policy that can affect significant factors. Because regional government structures are rarely available to match regional economies, policy analysis necessarily must turn to the subregional level—to local governments. Local governments might or might not collaborate well across a region; for example, regions with a diversity of local governments face greater probabilities that local actors will engage in competition, rather than in collaboration. Nevertheless, as the policymaking units that comprise regions, cities and other local governments are appropriate units of analysis.

In examining the relationship between the technology economy and cities, I look at two prominent issues in local economic development. The primary goal of local economic development is tied to jobs and the businesses that house those jobs. Depending on a city's situation, the goal can be to retain local businesses that are important to the local economy as well as support growth and spin-offs of these businesses. Many cities also enter into the economic development market of attracting business from other locations to their city's jurisdiction. Often the policies seeking business growth are designed to manipulate factors that are important to business. However, given the diversity of business operations, policies often favor certain types of businesses more than others. The technology economy is likely to have a differential effect on businesses, and understanding which businesses are more likely to benefit in the technology economy is consequential to localities wishing to capture the technology economy. This includes a greater understanding of technology infrastructure vis-à-vis these businesses, and how local policymakers can best utilize technology infrastructure for economic development.

I have confronted four challenges in analyzing the relationship between the technology economy and cities. First, as the explanation of the economic and technological trends highlighted, observers, scholars, and analysts have yet to describe the phenomena in comprehensive and parsimonious fashion. Most of us are aware that changes are occurring, but we lack sufficient understanding to offer precise definitions or descriptions of what we are observing. A second challenge is that analyses have not been conducted at the local level. Most of the existing research focuses on the regional analysis, or interregional comparison. As a result, there is a need for intraregional analysis and figuring out what is occurring at the subregional level. A third challenge, which results from the second challenge, is that we do not know what local governments, as policymaking entities, are doing to facilitate technology economy growth in their jurisdictions, except perhaps anecdotally. Finally, the lack of systematic, comparative research on cities leads to questionable policy advice, or a lack of advice, about strategies cities should pursue in seeking to be active in the technology economy.

A Local Technology Economy Framework

This book analyzes the role of cities relative to large economic changes and technology infrastructure. The following questions guide the analysis:

1. What is the technology economy?
2. Which cities are performing well or not so well in the technology economy, and what are the characteristics of these cities?
3. What are cities doing in the technology economy arena in terms of attracting growth and developing infrastructure?
4. Are there local strategies or advice that can be used to better craft policies targeting technology economy growth?

In addressing these questions, I attempt to provide needed insight into the impact of technology on local economies, to inform the policy discourse about this arena of work, and suggest strategies to help cities position themselves more effectively in the technology economy.

What Is the Technology Economy?

The first step in this research is to provide some context regarding the trends in economic and technological change. Previous examinations of economic change (high-tech or information economy) have been too sector-focused. I argue that the technology economy is reliant on both the sectors that are leading economic growth and the technology infrastructure as the foundation that makes innovation and growth possible. The technology economy is composed of two distinct, yet interrelated building blocks. First, the technology sectors are those industries that both employ key workers and generate technology-related goods and services. These industries invest heavily in research and development while employing individuals in occupations that require more years of formal education, training, and work experience. The second building block is the technology infrastructure, not unlike the core physical infrastructure of highways, roads, and water lines; however, information technology and telecommunications networks have a smaller and somewhat less visible footprint in comparison. Technology infrastructure is a key input as well as a foundation for economic growth because of its capacity for innovation and change. For technology sectors, technology infrastructure reinforces growth and innovation capacities, and these sectors are often also responsible for transforming and developing better technology solutions as inputs and final products in the economy. In other words, the technology economy sectors need technology infrastructure to operate, and those sectors then develop new technologies and infrastructure as product and services. The cycle of technology infrastructure innovation is key to the success of technology sectors as well as the technology economy. This book offers a view of the trends affecting economic change by linking technology industries to technology infrastructure in the technology economy.

Myriad and complex interrelationships between the technology sectors and technology infrastructure suggest that the effect of the technology economy has both macro- and micro-level impacts. At the macro level, global, national, and regional trends in technology sectors and infrastructure are important in setting the landscape. Both national and subnational governments have an interest in the technology economy's well-being, yet the U.S. government's policy action in both technology sectors and infrastructure development is, to date, better characterized as sporadic and inadequate. Industrial policy is absent, and as the major proponent of rules for infrastructure in the United States, the Federal Communications Commission has consciously left technology infrastructure development and deployment in the hands of the private sector. The United States remains the only country in the Group of 8 countries that does not have a national broadband plan. Other countries outside the

Group of 8, like Australia, Singapore, Malaysia, South Korea, Estonia, and India, also have national broadband strategies.

At the subnational level, state, regional, and local governments all have a role to play in the technology economy. In terms of state governments in the United States, policy actions tend to be more regional in focus and rely heavily on local government participation. The local level matters. Local policymakers are key public sector actors because cities and counties are the building blocks of regions and regional economies. The lack of regional governmental structures in the United States positions local officials as the key policymaking actors in the region, designing and implementing policies that create opportunities for localities and individuals across the region. Consequently, this book focuses on cities as key local governments that shape policies in response to the technological change. This is not to say that studying other levels of government is inappropriate or not of interest, but given the role of local policymakers in this policy arena, there is a need to better understand what is happening at the city level. For example, are great disparities apparent across cities in terms of the technology economy? To what extent are the disparities a function of different levels of technology infrastructure investment and capacity? Cities that lack technology infrastructure could be at a relative disadvantage, creating a spatial digital divide. As coined by Larry Irving of the Department of Commerce's National Telecommunications and Information Administration, the term "digital divide" commonly refers to Internet access inequity or unfairness among individuals. But it is also important to recognize that a digital divide exists in spatial terms, among places, and that place often determines whether or not individuals have access to technologies. A city's technology infrastructure is ground zero for determining Internet access in communities and capacities available for all economic sectors of the city. Beyond Internet access, many firms and government entities may require access to high-capacity, dedicated telecommunications lines. The existence of adequate technology infrastructure not only affects the digital divide among people, but it also affects places' or cities' abilities to attract firms that require such infrastructure relative to other places. Similar to how the railroad lines produced both boomtowns and ghost towns in the nineteenth century, depending upon whether the line came through a location or not, technology infrastructure impacts the future vitality of places. The pitting of localities with superior technology infrastructure against those that lack it emphasizes the disparities created in a private market, where greater return on investment opportunities dictates the areas in which infrastructure development and capacity occur. The cycle of better infrastructure, where demand for it is higher, produces a situation that is ripe for public policy action, targeting disparities exacerbated by inequitable market mechanics.

Which Cities Are Performing Well or Not So Well in the Technology Economy, and What Are the Characteristics of These Cities?

Determining which cities are performing well in the technology economy and the characteristics of those cities is a means of diagnosing the disparities, that is, what factors are likely to promote success or less than ideal outcomes. Most of the research on technology economy sectors ranks regions or metropolitan areas based on relative strength in those sectors (Chapple et al. 2004; Progressive Policy Institute 2000; Atkinson and Gottlieb 2001; Sommers and Carlson 2000; American Electronics Association 1998; Cortright and Mayer 2001). In regard to technology infrastructure, the regional rankings for Internet backbone capacity or access points do not identify the gaps within a metropolitan area (Moss and Townsend 2000; Gorman 2002; Gorman and Malecki 2002). Regional rankings, while allowing for relative comparisons of regions, do not suggest why the differences exist or allow policymakers to identify specific areas of need. Using the city as the unit of analysis allows for additional insights into intraregional trends, while relying upon a similar methodology. For consistency, I examine the rankings of cities based on technology sector performance, which allows for a comparison of the technology economy's sectors to what are often called "high-tech," "new," or "information" economies. As a result of some overlap, the city analysis reveals which cities of the well-ranked regions, like the Silicon Valley, may be shouldering the region's performance. In addition to the rankings, I identify a range of socioeconomic characteristics and technology infrastructure measures to determine how they are correlated with differential technology sector performance. The analysis points to education, innovation, and youth populations as being important local factors, and it provides evidence that technology infrastructure is significant at the local level. Overall, the method of ranking cities and exploring defining characteristics suggests that there is a need for local government policy that can generate leading technology environments.

What Are Cities Doing in the Technology Economy Arena in Terms of Attracting Growth and Developing Infrastructure?

Local government policy remains one of the most diverse policy arenas, a function of more than 35,000 separate units of local government that operate under fifty different state government structures. Understanding how cities (19,429 of these local governments) are attempting to create or fit into the technology economy is paramount. The largest barrier to analyzing policies at the local level is a lack of quality information. In the face of diverse policy actions and a large number of local governments, we lack comparative, large sample analyses at the city level. As a result, many who examine local government issues turn to case studies and anecdotal evidence, approaches that provide contextual insight through thick description but present problems in terms of broad generalization. In addition to case studies that supplement the analysis presented in this book, I utilize survey data to uncover how cities are addressing technology economy issues, in particular the role of technology infrastructure development in the city vis-à-vis technology sectors and other municipal concerns.

The survey analysis reveals that cities are sensitive to the changing tides of their local economies, and it shows the importance of technology infrastructure in current and future economic stability. Yet this recognition has limited influence on local policies concerned with economic development because of three major hurdles. The first is that most local officials interested in technology infrastructure assessment and development are often operating in conflict with their local private infrastructure providers. Private providers often decline to increase capacity in response to government requests and even refuse to share information about the capacity of available local infrastructure because they are sensitive to competition in the local market. These public-private conflicts of interest lead to the second hurdle—a lack of infrastructure knowledge and capacity at the local level. Unlike the superior records that most cities have on core infrastructures like roads and water and utility lines, the technology infrastructure is a relative unknown in terms of location and capacity. Although some entrepreneurial cities have collected this information through permitting processes, those that possess this information are few. This fact leads to the third hurdle—that public-private conflicts and lack of information about technology infrastructure preclude the use of the information as part of economic development strategies. It is difficult to identify gaps and needs without the information about location and capacity. These three hurdles underscore the disconnection between actual policies and the recognition of the technology economy's role in the future economic viability of cities.

The public-private infrastructure problem is playing out in both federal and state courts, as well as state legislatures. The intent of the federal Telecommunications Act of 1996 was to increase competition in allowing any entity to have fair access to other private provider's networks (Telecommunications Act of 1996). The underlying theory was that as competition increased, more providers would build and make improvements to their existing infrastructure. However, many local governments found that their cities were not selected as areas that would provide the return on investment that most incumbent or new competitive providers required. Cities that were unable to take advantage of technology infrastructure because of conflicts with the private sector, or that were aware of their disadvantage relative to neighboring jurisdictions, have sought to solve the infrastructure issue through the public domain. Local officials describe the process of creating advanced technology infrastructures across a community, regardless of income, race, or type of business, as a public service because unlike federal laws governing telephone service, no laws ensure universal service of broadband or any other infrastructure capacity. The result is many gaps in service and underserved areas. A recent U.S. Supreme Court ruling concerning the cities in Missouri proved to be a setback for these "activist cities" (*Nixon v. Missouri Municipal League* 2004). Local authorities in Missouri sought to become telecommunications providers in their cities, but the state's attorney general took the position that the Telecommunications Act of 1996 did not overrule the state's law forbidding cities in Missouri to offer those services. The Supreme Court agreed. Although a number of states already had laws explicitly forbidding a locality to enter into the telecommunications business, since the Supreme Court ruling, the private telecommunications industry has used the Missouri decision to lobby numerous state legislatures for laws that forbid or limit a municipality's ability to build and finance telecommunications infrastructure networks and/or offer services.[4] If these proposed and enacted laws do not prevent localities from engaging in infrastructure development, they often include multiple roadblocks: giving local private providers the right of first refusal in providing better infrastructure to the city before planning a local option; requiring approval for a project through a local referendum; enforcing that the project be financed with general obligation bonds, instead of revenue bonds that would be paid off from the infrastructure project's revenues; and restricting the city's ability to lease or sell the built infrastructure capacity at rates below private sector rates. Similar efforts are ongoing at the federal level.[5] All of these requirements serve to keep cities out of a very important policy arena. Similar to the interaction between traditional infrastructure and economic development, cities in the technology economy need to have some ability to influence and control the development of infrastructure that is associated with new sources of economic growth.

The arguments for and against local telecommunications activities point to a vast gap in understanding. The opponents of local rights declare that the public sector should not be allowed to compete with the private sector for the same service provision. Ironically, most local public officials agree that they should not supersede private activities. The problem for local officials comes in the fact that the level and quality of service in regard to advanced telecommunications infrastructure, such as broadband services, is either not available or only sporadically covers neighborhoods where private providers believed demand would not be high enough to warrant their investment. In both situations, local officials claim that it is their public duty to provide services when there are disparities, and where local needs go unmet. Adequate, advanced technology infrastructure is in the public interest because it is linked to municipal quality of life, economic well-being, and the city's future vitality. Preclusion of a city's ability to address these infrastructure problems effectively locks in the disparities created by the market.

Are There Local Strategies or Advice That Can Be Used to Better Craft Policies Targeting Technology Economy Growth?

The lessons of city-level analysis, from the survey analysis and case studies, points to specific policy goals and actions that cities might use in the technology economy. Unlike strategy and policy advice based on regional comparisons, anecdotes, or only industry-specific analyses, the collected body of evidence in this research points to improved understanding of local decisions vis-à-vis the technology economy. The local-level analysis is important to understanding trends at the regional level

(Kotkin 2000; Barnes and Ledebur 1998; Florida 2002). Emphasis on technology infrastructure from a local economic development perspective helps to bridge the gaps for local governments more likely to look at technology infrastructure from a technical, architectural, or urban planning point of view (Mitchell 1996; Graham 1999; Computer Systems Policy Project 1998). Currently, in regard to infrastructure, a disconnection exists at the local policy level, due not only to a lack of examination and recognition of the importance of cities, but also to the fact that the role of technology infrastructure in local planning is often isolated from a natural partner—economic development. Are localities that ignore or are unaware of technology infrastructure's importance to economic development and the municipal quality of life falling through the net? Developing technology infrastructure through local economic development strategies and policies has the potential to yield growth in technology sectors, innovation, education, and human capital. The research presented here about the technology economy's relationship to cities is grounded in local experiences that will hopefully provide appropriate advice and lessons for policymakers.

Three Approaches to Studying Cities

One of the most difficult problems to deal with in any examination of cities and their local governments is the paucity of comparative data. At the national level, the U.S. Census is a prevalent data source for many, providing local government finance, government employment, population statistics, and business patterns information on a regular basis over time. Although a needed source, the U.S. Census data present three problems for those wanting to analyze local government conditions. First, for much of the local government data only local governments in cities with populations over 25,000 are included in much of the substantive data collection. Given that about 90 percent of all local governments fall below this threshold, detailed facts are missing for rural areas and for many smaller and growing cities in metropolitan and "micropolitan" areas. The second problem is that some local governments do not respond regularly to substantive census questionnaires. In the case of the Census of Governments, cities like Mesa, Arizona (the fortieth largest U.S. city by population in 2003), Champaign, Illinois, and Rochester, Minnesota, did not provide government finances data in 1992; nor did Lakewood, Colorado, Gary, Indiana, and Champaign, Illinois, in 1997;

nor Camden, New Jersey, Centennial, Colorado, and Moline, Illinois, in 2002, as just a few examples. Most of these cities are among the larger cities in their states and regions, and their position in their regional economies makes their conditions important to capture in comparative analyses. The third problem for researchers interested in local conditions is that national-level data collections do not capture specific policies or policy issues. Data are not collected, for instance, on whether local governments utilize policies such as tax incentives for economic development. These three problems should not be interpreted as criticisms of the U.S. Census. In most instances, the U.S. Census is the lone source for much of the comparative data available for localities. The available data cannot possibly cover the range of conditions in localities, let alone policy actions. Nevertheless, the lack of local-level data hampers assessments of conditions and development of policy options. This book uses national-level data, where available, to analyze the characteristics of cities that are leading or lagging in technology economy industry.

As a result of the paucity and shortcomings of nationally collected local comparative data, research on cities often turns to case studies that enable an in-depth look at local government actions, strategies, and conditions. Case studies are able to concentrate on the exact interrelationships of interest and provide a greater contextual understanding of many phenomena. Although offering a complementary method to analyzing national-level data, the cases are often selected based on their achievement, or lack thereof, on a given indicator. The selection method decreases the likelihood of generalizing the findings to other local governments and forgoes any national comparison. Regardless, case study methodologies provide contextual information where other sources of data are unavailable or inadequate. This book explores the technology economy in seven cities, focusing on each city's planning and strategies with respect to the technology economy.

The questions of this book, however, require more than reliance upon national-level data sources and case studies because the effects of the technology economy are diverse and complex, and some observers may question the impact the technology economy is having on local economies nationwide. The effects of technology infrastructure and sectors, separately and jointly, require comparisons of a larger sample of local governments. Survey research is one method that can address analysis of larger samples while filling the gaps of case studies or national-level data collections with both policy and local context from a national cross-section of cities. Survey research is also appropriate for the subject matter of this book because the data on technology infrastructure are proprietary and often unavailable at the local level in any robust format, necessitating going directly to local governments for information. Survey data collection provides the opportunity to gain a snapshot of what local governments are doing in regard to technology infrastructure and how it relates to their planning and strategies. Querying local governments on what they know about their infrastructure, from quantity to quality, conveys local technology infrastructure capacity from a local government perspective; that is, although a city may have abundant private fiber-optic networks and wireless network towers, the local government may be unaware of its relative position in comparison to other cities in the region and/or may not be thinking of this infrastructure as an asset that could be leveraged for economic growth. Another local government may be relatively worse off, but very aware that it is lacking infrastructure and doing everything in its power to change the situation, through partnerships or through its own development and deployment of technology infrastructure. In addition, survey data collection sets the landscape of where a representative sample of cities and their local governments are in the technology economy, not just in terms of technology infrastructure. Local government awareness of capacities with respect to the technology economy may provide clearer policymaking strategies in the long run. The lack of reliable data sources regarding technology infrastructure and local strategies of economic development calls for direct data collection as the source for its relationships in the technology economy.

Survey research is not without problems. Although it offers some insight into local context, possible anecdotes, and national-level comparison, survey research has shortcomings that include bias in terms of the respondent and nonrespondent issues, and is able to capture a picture of circumstances at only one point in time. In regard to bias, a local official may be more likely to respond to a survey that is of personal interest or about a subject that is of greater concern in the city at that point in time, and unlikely to respond in an arena where her city is less involved or performing less well. In addition, responding local officials are likely to portray their cities' situation in a more positive light in an effort to rank or score well in given indices. Nevertheless, where other data sources do not exist or have significant gaps, survey research is an efficient method for conducting larger sample comparisons. In particular, survey research is used quite often in research on local economic development policy and conditions.[6] Similarly, this book uses a survey of local economic development officials in cities to supplement existing national-level data and case-study research.

In an effort to gain a better understanding of conditions and to craft better policy, this book uses a triangulation of methods, drawing on national-level data analysis, survey analysis, and case studies to provide a clearer picture of the technology economy in cities. Lack of information leads to less optimal policy advice, such as the use of old policies for new problems (for example, tax incentives) versus the use of new policies for new problems (for example, offering complete wireless networks in jurisdictions through public-private partnerships). The triangulation approach still carries the problems inherent in each individual method, but my hope is that this strategy lessens these while improving upon previous work and generating interest in producing, collecting, and sharing information on cities, technology, and local economies.

Using the framework and approaches outlined above, this books seeks to learn more about cities' actions relative to their current position in the technology economy. In Chapter 2, I develop the theoretical underpinnings of the technology economy. Navigating the relationship between economic change and technological infrastructure depends upon clearly delineating the technology economy from the various labels other analyses have offered in an attempt to capture the trends that the technology economy includes. Comparison of existing labels reveals what the technology economy is not, while also showing areas of overlap. Given that most of the labels focus on economic sectors, this comparison influences and guides the definition of technology industries, one building block of the technology economy. These industries rely upon innovation and human capital, the factors contributing to economic growth in the technology economy. I identify two sets of industries, one based on a human capital definition and called technology employers, and the other based on innovation, called technology generators. The technology economy also includes the technology infrastructure, the second building block, which enables much of the innovation propelling economic change. Technology infrastructure is an underlying foundation that is necessary to harness continued, long-term growth. In defining what the technology economy and its building blocks are, I develop measures of the building blocks and address several challenges to the definitions and data availability in terms of local-level analysis.

Chapter 3 presents an analysis of technology economy sectors in cities through a comparison of leading and lagging cities in terms of employment in both the technology employer industries and technology generator industries. This comparison, as well as a subsector breakdown of industries in each sector by product and service, reveals that technology economy industries cluster regionally, similar to the regional clusters identified in other technology-related analyses. It also highlights cities that are more likely to have advantages in human capital or innovation. The analysis follows with an examination of city characteristics, including technology infrastructure, for cities performing at differential rates in the technology economy. Statistical analysis points to a series of factors, including technology infrastructure, as having a differential effect on cities' performance relative to technology economy sectors. I analyze the overall effect of these factors on city technology sectors with several regression models. The findings show that cities with a greater presence in technology sectors have younger populations, higher rates of innovation, higher incomes, and are more economically advantaged. In addition, cities that integrate technology infrastructure as part of local economic development strategies are also more likely to have a technology sector advantage.

With a better understanding of what an advantaged technology economy city looks like, Chapter 4 examines the role of the technology economy in cities with respect to economic development policies. Utilizing survey data, I present perspectives from city officials in terms of local conditions, the role of the technology economy and its sectors in local economies, and technology infrastructure capacity. The private sector's control of infrastructure location and capacity rules out any comprehensive, aggregate data source for this analysis; thus, the survey provides a unique opportunity to assess local technology infrastructure from the perspective of local officials. Local economic development officials reported that technology infrastructure plays a key role in their economies, and their cities are often providers of this strategic asset. However, cities are not the main providers, as this is a role that city officials say is held by private actors. The conflict between the public and private sectors regarding further development and location of technology infrastructure in their jurisdictions presents major challenges to cities wanting to integrate technology infrastructure into policies and strategies. Consequently, many cities lack knowledge about the capacity and location of their local technology infrastructure, hampering the design of adequate strategies for local growth and future development.

In Chapter 5 I examine the technology economy in entrepreneurial cities, focusing on each city's planning and strategies with respect to the technology infrastructure and sectors. These entrepreneurial cities are overcoming the issues of conflict with the private sector, yet moving in a direction of attaining greater information about their local economy vis-à-vis technology. Each of these cities utilizes its technology infrastructure as an asset, whether it be through creating and maintaining an inventory on the location, capacity, and ownership of all technology infrastructure; incorporating and formulizing the role of technology and telecommunications into economic development planning documents; or using technology infrastructure as a specific policy device. Each city has crafted a role for technology infrastructure with the intent of positive economic development returns, and in many cases has designed strategies to create, retain, and attract technology sectors appropriate for its economy. Consequently, these cities demonstrate a holistic policy approach that puts them in a position of strength in the technology economy.

I conclude in Chapter 6 with a reflection on the factors contributing to local advantages in the technology economy and the policy learning that is possible from this local-level analysis. With a greater understanding of what the technology economy means and holds for cities, a set of policy options and strategies is presented to help guide future policymaking and economic development efforts in cities. In addition, a number of anecdotes from the survey research and case studies provide examples of how cities are moving specific focuses on one aspect of the technology economy to broader approaches aimed at linking the technology economy to economic vitality and municipal livability.

In essence, I argue that the future vitality of cities is attached to the future of the technology economy. Understanding what cities need to be prepared to meet ongoing economic and technological changes is essential to future growth. The exploration of technology infrastructure and technology sectors at the local level provides some guidance for cities seeking to harness this relatively new source of economic growth.

2

Defining the Technology Economy

> Although there is now a substantial body of literature on the role of information technology in the economy, much of it is inconclusive.
>
> —*Erik Brynjolfsson and Brian Kahin*

> Our remote ancestors did not expand their economics much by simply doing more of what they had already been doing. . . . They expanded their economics by adding new kinds of work. So do we. Innovating economies expand and develop.
>
> —*Jane Jacobs*

Prior to my examination of what the technology economy holds for cities, I must first define what the technology economy is. Presumably, cities focus on how technology economy–centered economic development policy can lead to a stronger, more diversified economic base, helping to secure cities' future economic viability. Beyond economic growth, cities' investment in the technology economy can be seen as improving municipal livability through better delivery of government services, expanding educational opportunities, and decreasing the spatial digital divide. Therefore, it is important to define the technology economy in order to examine the extent of cities' roles in this economy. While the technology economy and its many variants—"new economy," "information economy," "high-tech economy," to name just a few—may seem to be a familiar terms, certain assumptions are embedded in each label and each individual label does not necessarily describe or refer to the same phenomenon as the other. Reflecting on the multitude of labels and ideas surrounding global, macroeconomic, and technological changes is essential to better understand where we are headed. This is certainly true for local governments seeking to target their investments to yield optimum growth and spillover benefits from these changes.

Popular and academic analyses of the changes in the economy over the past few decades are broad and sometimes inconsistent; however, start with the same three points. The first point is that the U.S. economy is gradually shifting from being goods-based to service-based, as well as knowledge- or information-based. The goods-to-services shift has been well documented. From 1960–2002, as a percentage of wages and salaries earned in the United States, the goods sector declined from 42 percent to 16 percent. Meanwhile, the services sector increased from 22 percent to 38 percent. Over the same period, as a percentage of total consumption in the United States, the goods sector declined from 59 percent to 41 percent and the services sector inversely increased from 41 percent to 59 percent (all consumption is either for goods or services) (Tannenwald 2004). Robert Tannenwald cautions against the misperception that consumers now purchase more services and fewer goods, arguing that consumers purchase more goods than before—for example, most Americans now own more than one television set (a good) whereas they had only one TV set in 1960. What has changed is that the price of goods is relatively lower as a result of global economic competition and technological innovation. The prices of services, on the other hand, and the quantity of services consumed, are higher. For example, most cellular phone services today provide the good—the phone—free of charge or for a relatively small price, but charge customers for the use of the service (charges that accrue monthly and amount to well more than the cost of producing the phone). Consumers are therefore acquiring more goods, but paying relatively more, in total, for services.

The economic shift is not limited to the change from a goods- to a services-based economy. The more recent move is toward a knowledge- or information-based economy. In an effort to measure the impact of this, Tannenwald points to the rise in the ratio of intangible assets—patents, databases, software, formulas, and trademarks—to tangible assets (Tannenwald 2004). For all industries, this ratio increased from less than 1 percent to 18 percent between 1977 and 1997. For individual sectors, the ratio of intangible assets to tangible assets may be higher or lower—25 percent for the services sector for example, compared to 7 percent for retail trade—but the increase over the twenty-year period has been substantial for all sectors. Similarly, but using different definitions, Florida argues that the world economy is undergoing an economic transformation akin to the industrial revolution—moving from economies where growth is driven by goods and services sectors to economies where growth is driven by innovation and creativity (Florida 2002). Using an occupation-based definition to look at the rise of what he calls the creative class of workers, Florida found that this class comprised more than 30 percent of the economy in 1999 (Florida 2002).

The second major point of economic change is that globalization of markets pressures all countries to evaluate how to efficiently adapt to global, as opposed to national, regional, or local, competition. Competitiveness in the global economy also requires subnational regions to balance these requirements with other local requirements (Barnes and Ledebur 1998). In fact, "the same forces of globalization that have reshaped our industrial system are acting on these cities and regions" (Florida 2005b, 10). Local adaptation and restructuring to address these challenges affects local policy choices as well as options (Clarke and Gaile 1998).

Third, the use of new technologies is not limited to advances in production processes and basic business operations, but it is also leading to the creation and growth of new industry sectors (Jorgenson and Stiroh 2000; Jorgenson 2001; Oliner and Sichel 2000; Kling and Lamb 2000). For example, the Internet has led to the development of businesses like Internet service providers (ISPs), website hosts, and web search portals, none of which existed before the 1990s. Recognizing these three points, most researchers and pundits seek to explain what the culmination of these trends means for the future of the nation's economic competitiveness and growth. Although all three trends are important, I concentrate on the third, not because it is necessarily more important, but because it provides the greatest possibility of addressing the policymaking access point from a local government perspective. Technology infrastructure and the attraction of technology-oriented industry is the point where local policymakers are most likely to be currently involved and most likely to have an effect—as opposed to affecting large-scale macroeconomic changes in the global economy.

Unpacking the Labels

The news media, research reports, and numerous books have attempted to describe technology's effect on business and have given it myriad conflicting labels and definitions (Rondinelli 2001; Cairncross 1995; U.S. Department of Commerce, Office of Technology Assessment 1995; Castells 1989; Malecki 1991; Moss 1998; Gorman 2002; Forman, Goldfarb, and Greenstein 2004; Elstrom et al. 1997; Porter 1998). The labels most commonly used include "new economy," "high-tech economy," "information economy," and "digital economy." Unfortunately, these competing and ambiguously used labels lead to further confusion among policymakers seeking to address these challenges. Although each label generally refers to a dramatic shift in the production of goods and services, in a strict interpretation, each of these labels describes a different phenomenon. One label describes macroeconomic change, and the other three are really labels for industries or sets of industries, based on different criteria.

Perhaps the most overutilized label, the "new economy," is actually a macroeconomic construct used to describe the overall economy in the 1990s, a period when rapid economic growth and productivity coexisted with low inflation and low unemployment rates (Kling and Lamb 2000). Much of the 1990s economic growth coincided, and was in part driven by, the rise of technology-producing industries and firms, such as Intel (microprocessors), Microsoft (software), and Cisco (network routers and switches), or technology-using industries and firms, such as eBay (online auctions) and Amazon.com (online retail sales). Some have even associated the organizational and cultural values of these firms with the new economy (Bresnahan and Gambardella 2004). Thus, the new economy is often viewed as synonymous with the diffusion of technological innovation through organizations and economic markets. While technology and innovation contributed substantially to the new economy, the label itself is not limited to growth in technology sectors, industries, or firms. The ambiguity surrounding the label has led to charges that the label *new economy* does not really refer to anything at all (Florida 2005c).

The remaining commonly used labels are associated with specific industries or sets of industries. For several decades now, analysts have studied a set of "high-tech" industries because the growth of these industries was seen as a key driver of economic growth, and the industries themselves therefore were seen as possible targets for economic development (Markusen, Hall, and Glasmeier 1986; DeVol 1999; Glasmeier 1991; Scott 1993). A high-tech industry is usually defined by either its greater-than-average intensity in science and technical occupations, or its research and development expenditures (Malecki 1997). The technique of employing these possible definitions has varied in execution. While high-tech industries are defined based on their employees or their expenditures on research, "digital economy" industries are defined by their physical technology inputs in the production process. Digital economy industries produce "goods or services whose development, production, sale, or provision is critically dependent upon digital technologies" (Kling and Lamb 2000, 297). A sector bearing yet another popular label, the "information economy" is concerned with industries whose output is technology. The label *information economy* describes the workings of information technology–producing industries ranging from those that produce hardware (such as Intel) and software (such as Microsoft) to those that produce all "informational goods and services, including publishing, entertainment, research, legal and insurance services, and teaching in all forms" (Kling and Lamb 2000, 297). Information economy industries have grown as a component of the economy, such that information technology–producing industries accounted for nearly one-third of economic growth in the United States between 1995 and 2000. Despite the economic downturn, information technology–producing industries were estimated to contribute to over one-third of U.S. economic growth in 2003 (U.S. Department of Commerce, Economic Statistics Administration 2003).

Unfortunately, no one label systematically describes the combination of economic growth and transformation, the resultant industrial composition, and the supporting technologies that make these changes possible. Consequently, each label provides an incomplete story, missing the interrelationships between the economy, industry, and infrastructure. As an alternative, I use the label "technology economy." The following sections lay out the key elements, or building blocks, of the technology economy and how it interacts with local economic development policy.

Building Blocks of the Technology Economy

Much of what analysts have come to identify as comprising the technology economy relies heavily on two specific and distinct elements—the building blocks of the technology economy. One building block is associated with technology, but more specifically, information technology and telecommunications. How our society has absorbed and increased its reliance upon these technologies sponsors a variety of viewpoints, including reports of significant impacts on the daily lives of individuals, organizations, businesses, and governments. I refer to these technologies as the infrastructure of the technology economy. The second building block of the technology economy focuses on the economic sectors, industries, and businesses that are likely to be dependent on, or to produce, the infrastructure of the technology economy. As the discussion of labels reveals, the definition of sectors and industries varies for high-tech, information technology, and digital technology, and these distinctions are consequential to this research. What follows is a detailed explanation of each of these building blocks of the technology economy.

Infrastructure of the Technology Economy

In describing the framework of the technology economy, the building block most necessary is the infrastructure; it is the foundation for the technology economy, just as physical, public infrastructure like roads, bridges, water supply facilities, sewers, airports, mass transit, and electric and gas plants are for traditional economic and social interactions. The infrastructure of the technology economy is, in essence, as integral to the growth of that economy as railroads were to the industrial revolution or the interstate highway system, ports, and airports to the transport of goods today. The technology economy's infrastructure has two essential components—information technology and telecommunications. Unfortunately, most analyses do not make a distinction between the two components and use them interchangeably.

Information technology refers to applied computer systems, including computer hardware, software programs, computer networking, and the consulting services to support the use and implementation of information technology. Within the context of a business or enterprise, information technologies aid communications and handle information processing, which is to convert, store, process, transmit, and retrieve information. Information technology is really an *internal* component of infrastructure, just like any input or machine that enables a production process, which suggests an answer to the question of why information technology has such a powerful role in the technology economy. As an input, information technology capital has a dual role as it mixes with labor and non–information technology capital in the production process —enabling improvements in the process, as in the case of a software program being utilized to computerize billing—or it can lead to greater efficiencies through a coordination effect, reducing the costs, or increasing the capacity of communications within a business or between businesses, for example (Dedrick, Gurbaxani, and Kraemer 2003). The application and use of information technology often leads to changes in the production or business process through the introduction of new managerial practices, organizational structures, and innovative methods of producing the same or new products and services. While aggregate investment in information technology increased from 9 percent to 22 percent of total U.S. capital investment during the 1990s, not all firms are able to utilize or choose to utilize information technology at the same rate. These disparities have productivity consequences. Firms with greater levels of investment in information technology during the 1990s had labor productivity rates that were more than four times larger than firms with comparatively little invested in information technology (Council of Economic Advisors 2001; Jorgenson and Stiroh 2000; Oliner and Sichel 2002; Stiroh 2001a, 2001b).

The second component of technology economy infrastructure is telecommunications. Telecommunications involves the encoded transmission of voice, data, and video via electrical, optical, or wireless means over a range of distance between computers or network processors (Goldman and Rawles 2003). Unlike information technology, telecommunications is not a relatively new technology, but the evolution of telecommunications as a technology and as an industry is why telecommunications is an essential component of the technology economy's infrastructure. Over the past forty years, telecommunications networks have become an increasingly important infrastructure. During the 1960s, private telecommunications providers invested heavily in the expansion of telecommunications infrastructure, resulting in technological improvements that increased fiber-optic cable's capacity to carry more data at faster rates and led to greater deployment, in terms of miles and geography. These and other continuing developments have significantly reduced the cost of telecommunications as an input in economic production (Cronin, Hebert, and Colleran 1992; Cronin et al. 1993). Telecommunications infrastructure is often referred to as a component of, or synonymous with, information technology. However, telecommunications networks are *external* to business processes and operations, provided outside of the individual firm by other private sector or public sector (such as cities) agents.

Current communications ultimately depend upon the existence of telecommunications networks, whether it is voice communications over telephones, visual video communications, or data communications of e-mails and other nonvoice/nonvideo traffic. The state of the networks carrying these communications, or the telecommunications infrastructure, across cities varies greatly with the population density of the area. Although urban areas are often thought to possess adequate infrastructure, prior investment trends of telecommunications providers have given less priority to the growing demand for bandwidth—larger communication channels that can carry more information—in larger cities. In the case of fiber-optic networks, telecommunications providers have traded off greater investment in metropolitan area networks, which transmit data out of the city, for greater investment in long-haul networks that transmit data over long-distance networks between cities. According to Susan Walcott and James Wheeler (2001, 321), "Hair-thin threads of glass utilizing laser light pulses in digital computer code, with multiple glass fibers in each cable—some sending messages from A to B and others from B to A—are the standard physical paths for global Internet telecommunications for major numeric data and word and graphic information." In 2000, the Dell'Oro Group estimated a $7.5 to $15 billion investment preference for long-haul networks (Ames 2001). The economic slowdown of 2001 flattened out investment patterns for long-haul networks, such that RHK estimated the 2001 long-haul market at $5.6 billion and metro market at $4.8 billion (RHK 2002). Yet there is proof that demand for long-haul networks is exceeding supply because prices are still high as "trade in raw materials and manufacture goods has been eclipsed by flows of goods, capital, and information" (Knox 1996, 115). As a result, cities are still struggling to gain more bandwidth, but fiber-optic networks may not be the only solution.

In 1990, analysts viewed telecommunications as the new urban infrastructure of economic growth (Schmandt, Williams, and Strover 1990), but this focus was misguided because it stressed the importance of long-distance calling rates and ignored the largest growth area of business, data, and network requirements. New business requirements and the telecommunications networks that were needed to meet these needs fueled much of the late-1990s growth. However, while often referred to in a generic way, telecommunications networks are diverse and differ in the capacity and speed with which they carry voice, video, and data. Recognizing these distinctions is important if cities are going to play a role in infrastructure planning in order to meet the needs of local businesses and citizens.

The largest distinction is that some telecommunications networks require physical cables, which is referred to as wire line service, and others operate without wires and are known as wireless. Each type of network offers telecommunications solutions for the transmission of voice, video, and data. Wire line services can carry the "triple play" of voice, video, and data transmissions or traffic. In comparison, wireless technologies are currently only available for voice and data applications. Wire line voice networks are the typical telephone services that local incumbent telecommunications providers, like Verizon in New York City, or Qwest in Phoenix, supply to residential and business customers. Wire line data service includes non-telephone-line transmissions of data across networks, using digital transmission links like T-1 (45 megabits per second) and other data transmission speeds. Businesses are the most likely customers, and the provider is most likely a long-haul data networking company like AT&T, Sprint, or Deutsche Telecom. However, this space is also filled with Internet service providers (ISPs) like Earthlink, AOL, AT&T, which are bringing greater bandwidth options to residential and small businesses, often referred to as broadband. DSL, or digital subscriber line, is one such technology that uses the traditional telephone lines but enables higher-speed Internet access than the standard modem connection over the same phone line. Many flavors of DSL technologies exist that dictate the maximum data transfer rates and whether communications upstream—from your computer to the ISP— and downstream—from the ISP to your computer—are at different speeds (asymmetrical) or at the same speed (symmetrical). Wire line video services are in the domain of the common cable TV or satellite company. For cable, companies like Comcast, Cox, or TCI provide video services and, due to recent upgrades of cable networks, even Internet and data communications services. These upgrades replaced all traditional coax networks with hybrid fiber coax networks, which use both optical fibers and coaxial cables and provide greater bandwidth capacity. These upgrades enabled cable companies to offer cable modem services, the main broadband competitor of voice companies' DSL solution. In regard to satellite services, companies like Echo Star, News Corp, Hughes Electronics, and TimeWarner provide not only video services but also data, voice, video, and Internet services to the defense and commercial sectors. The list of wire line technologies described is by no means comprehensive, but it does suggest the wide array of options that can quickly boggle a local policymaker's mind.

The wireless telecommunications services are no easier to size up. In terms of wireless options, voice communications are provided through the growing mobile or wireless voice markets from companies providing cellular phone services, such as Cingular, Verizon, and T-Mobile. The convergence of the wireless voice and wireless data services with special handsets creates even greater market penetration for these services, yet they are separate in function. Wireless data networks provide access to Internet and specialized data applications such as e-mail, instant messenger, text messaging, and web browsing; companies expanding in this market are BlackBerry, Verizon, NTT DoCoMo, and Richochet. Currently, the wireless data networks with substantial media in cities are WiFi (short for wireless fidelity) and WiMAX (worldwide interoperability for microwave access). These land-based wireless networks, as opposed to satellite-based wireless networks, have a number of applications, from networking a number of computers to share a residential or small-business internal broadband connection, to the popular WiFi "hot spots" or wireless Internet access points that provide free or moderately priced high-speed Internet access, to a possible future of an entire city being a hot spot.

Although these networks have experienced great success and have been municipally deployed in small public spaces in cities like Seattle and New York, many cities are looking to wireless networks as an opportunity to provide broadband access to all citizens and businesses. Currently, metro WiFi and WiMAX are the two best-positioned technologies. Metro WiFi uses networking technologies that enable all WiFi devices (computers, personal digital assistants, cell phones, or various other network appliances) using the data network to connect to the Internet. Chaska, Minnesota, for example, deployed a metro WiFi network in the summer of 2004, providing both in-home and outdoor broadband service to all of its citizens. However, due to WiFi's short-range capability, it requires many network routers and devices to ensure that access to the Internet covers large areas. Consequently, long-range WiMAX technologies are predicted to be a solution for low-density and large urban areas. WiMAX offers fixed-position, line-of-sight network with data rates up to 75 megabits per second for up to 30 miles, but WiMAX products are just starting to appear in the market. Cities in Korea are planning to deploy a WiMAX network in 2006, and the city of Philadelphia is the first large city in the United States planning to deploy a WiMAX network to provide high-speed access to its 135-square-mile area. In fact, Philadelphia recently awarded the contract for the citywide wireless network to Earthlink, a large ISP.

Telecommunications is an integral part of our technology economy, and cities and individuals continue to demand greater capacity and access opportunities. Although the private sector is the biggest investor in telecommunications, cities are increasingly exploring the possibility of their own telecommunications investments. Their interests range from those cities or areas that lack high-speed options to those with plenty of options. Smaller cities or rural areas often lack high-speed broadband access (cable modems or DSL) for residents and small businesses, or lack greater data transmission capacity options for large businesses. This divide often occurs because private telecommunications providers do not consider smaller cities or rural areas as providing an adequate return on telecommunications investment. Telecommunications investment "redlining," as this is sometimes labeled, has increased local government participation in developing and deploying telecommunications networks. Larger cities, like Philadelphia, Minneapolis, Denver, Boston, and Portland, Oregon, have a number of high-speed broadband and traditional telecommunications options but often find that many areas in their cities contain "dead zones" that lack high-speed telecommunications. All of these cities are exploring wireless networks that may be able to bridge the dead zones. Cities with significant broadband and telecommunications coverage are also exploring additional telecommunications deployment for the sake of maintaining a competitive position relative to other cities and areas. In general, cities at both ends of the spatial digital divide are increasingly recognizing that it is necessary for them to invest in information technology and telecommunications infrastructure. Because a growing number of technology infrastructure solutions are available, deciding on the technology that is right for an individual city requires understanding local needs with respect to the city's place in the technology economy.

Sectors of the Technology Economy

Although many analyses omit, confuse, or fail to adequately define the infrastructure of the technology economy, more confusion seems to surround the sectoral building block. Previous industrial definitions have used inputs, outputs, occupations, and expenditures as the basis for identifying technology industries, and each could be a valid measure of the industrial composition of the technology economy. However, the utilized sectoral definition should also relate to the first building block of the technology economy, its infrastructure. That is, what types of indus-

tries are highly dependent on this infrastructure? A review of the literature on technology's impact on industries examines a number of research studies indicating that an increased use of telecommunications
networks and investment in information technologies, such as computers and software, strengthens economic productivity (Dedrick, Gurbaxani, and Kraemer 2003). This dependency has had positive economic
and financial returns, such that firms with higher information technology investment from 1989 to 1999 have greater labor productivity rates
(Council of Economic Advisors 2001; Jorgenson and Stiroh 2000; Oliner
and Sichel 2002; Stiroh 2001a, 2001b). The firm-level and industry benefits aggregate into real macroeconomic gains. In general, economic
growth is possible through three basic mechanisms: "greater levels of
inputs (labor and capital), improved quality of the inputs, and greater
overall efficiency in the combination of inputs in production" (Dedrick,
Gurbaxani, and Kraemer 2003, 16). Many macroeconomic studies find
that information technology investment has major effects on U.S. labor
productivity growth, which increased from 1.5 percent in the period from
1973 to 1995 to 3.1 percent for the 1995–1999 period, and on gross
domestic product (GDP) growth, increasing from 3.0 percent to 4.8 percent for the same two periods (Council of Economic Advisors 2001;
Jorgenson 2001; Jorgenson and Stiroh 2000; Oliner and Sichel 2000).
Of these increases, information technology investment contributed one-
half of the GDP and labor productivity between 1995 and 1999 (Oliner
and Sichel 2000; Jorgenson and Stiroh 2000), but information technology capital investment has been contributing to U.S. real economic
growth for decades (Jorgenson, Ho, and Stiroh 2002). In fact, this growing body of research proclaims that these findings refute Robert Solow's
famous "productivity paradox," which claimed that high investment in
information technology, from computers, hardware, and software to telecommunications, seemed to produce no real economic gains.

The positive effect of information technology investment has altered
the business practices of all industries as they embraced the efficiencies
gained with incorporating information technology and telecommunications into production processes. The financial, insurance, and real estate
(FIRE) sector offers a perfect example, with telecommunications expenditures comprising more than 8 percent of all the spending in the
sector (Graham 1999). Telecommunications expenditures enable the
sector to more quickly and efficiently deliver many of their products or
services, such as fund transfers, credit cards, e-banking, mortgage loans,

and insurance quotes. Additionally, some of the FIRE sector is dependent on back-office job functions, and many of these routine and standardized operations can be decentralized into suburbs and small- and medium-sized towns because of telecommunications (Walcott and Wheeler 2001, 320). The substitution of face-to-face contact with telecommunications and information technologies is possible with certain occupations. However, not all industries will have similar investment patterns in information technology.

FIRE and wholesale and retail trade industries, for example, are information technology–investing or using industries, investing in much lower levels of information technology than a set of industries referred to as information technology producing. The information technology–producing industries include computer hardware and software and telecommunications technologies and services, and they are highly dependent upon the existence of technology economy infrastructure. Some have even grown and evolved out of the development and production of the infrastructure—electronic computers, hardware and communications equipment, computer software, and networking gear like high-end routers and switches that are integral in computer and telecommunications networks. Due to their high usage and production of information technology, information technology–producing industries accounted for one-third of U.S. economic growth in the 1990s and despite the 2001 recession continue to account for one-third of economic growth as well as 8 percent of U.S. GDP (U.S. Department of Commerce, Economic Statistics Administration 2003; Jorgenson 2001).

Studying either information technology–investing or information technology–producing firms depicts only part of the total effect of the technology economy. Although reliant on the technology economy's infrastructure, it is possible that neither type of firm will provide the single best target for cities. The diversity among information technology–investing firms in FIRE, durable goods manufacturing, retail and wholesale trade, and services might not allow local economic development practitioners the opportunity to focus on a particular set of industries with commonalities beyond information technology investment. In regard to information technology–producing industries, these industries are, by definition, only output based—a narrow set of industries that produce, process, or transmit information in the form of intermediate (goods and services that other industries use as inputs in their production processes) and final (for sale) goods and services. To better understand the technology economy, the definition of technology economy sectors must be tied to the infrastructure and the importance of the sectors to local economic development and growth. Much of the literature on economic development stresses the importance of developing industries that have innovative potential, resulting in spin-off companies, or require a higher-skilled workforce and educational base (Bresnahan and Gambardella 2004; Chapple et al. 2004; Eisinger 1988; Clarke and Gaile 1998). Skilled labor, rather than resources or physical capital, is human capital and is assumed to be a better driver of economic growth (Chapple et al. 2004). Economists such as Paul Romer, Paul Lucas, and Edward Glaeser share this opinion; they are all champions of new growth theory, which stresses the connection between human capital and economic growth (Romer 1986; Lucas 1988; Glaeser 1998, 2000). Richard Florida's recent definition of what he calls the creative class relies on human capital and its innovative capacity as the foundation for regional economic development—combining human capital, or talent, with technology and tolerance (Florida 2002). Commonly used definitions of technology-related industries do not have a direct relationship to human capital or a direct link to innovative capacity. There is a need for a new sectoral definition to capture a consequential relationship of the technology economy.

To clearly define the sectors of the technology economy, both human capital and innovation are considered, as in previous and well-accepted definitions of high-tech industry (Malecki 1997). However, the application of the definition has been updated to address changing data classifications. The change in the U.S. government classification system from the Standard Industrial Classification system (SIC) to the North American Industry Classification System (NAICS) in 1997 created a multitude of new classifications that did not directly relate to the old SIC categories; in other words, cross-walking between the NAICS and SIC classifications did not yield clean matches and resulted in exclusions of some important industries. The definitions have to be applied afresh under NAICS. Carnegie Mellon University's Center for Economic Development, with the State Science and Technology Institute (Paytas and Berglund 2004), recently published a set of technology definitions not only using the new NAICS, but also addressing two types of technology sectors, one based on human capital and the other on innovation. I use both NAICS-based definitions to identify the sectoral building block of the technology economy.

The first definition reflects human capital because it is an occupation-based methodology, using the Bureau of Labor Statistics Occupational Employment Statistics (OES) to determine the industries that have the highest concentration of science, engineering, and technical occupations. Examples of these occupations are engineering manager, chemical engineer, medical scientist, database administrator, and computer programmer. Use of these scientific occupations stresses the importance of a formal education, training, work experience, and related skills that an individual must possess to have such a job. All combine to build human capital. Chapple and co-authors (2004) most recently applied this methodology using 1998 OES data, selecting industries if their employment in science, technology, and engineering occupations exceeded three times the national average of 3.33 percent. However, this resulted in an SIC-defined technology industry (pre-NAICS). The Center for Economic Development applied the same methodology using 2002 OES data, which allowed them to cross-walk the selected industries to the NAICS industry employment criteria. The resulting group of technology industries from those criteria is used in this book to satisfy the technology economy's association with human capital. Examples of technology employer industries are semiconductor machinery manufacturing, aircraft manufacturing, Internet service providers and web search portals, and management, scientific, and technical consulting services. Although a scientific and technical workforce definition has been used in previous studies (Luker and Lyons 1997; Hadlock, Hecker, and Gannon 1991; Markusen, Hall, and Glasmeier 1986; Chapple et al. 2004), the definition used in this book is one of the initial attempts at using an updated and new NAICS-based definition, as well as being among the first to employ this analysis at the local level. For the sake of delineation, I refer to the scientific and technical definition of technology industries as "technology employers." Appendix A shows the NAICS industries that are technology employers.

A second innovation-based definition is necessary because technology employer industries do not account for all technology economy activity at the industrial level in the past two decades, nor does the definition directly address innovative capacity. The innovation definition selects industries that are generators of technological innovation, using the National Science Foundation's Survey of Industrial Research and Development for 2000 and the Center for Economic Development's criteria (National Science Foundation 2000). Selected industries must exceed the U.S. average for both research and development expenditures per employee ($11,297) and for the proportion of the full-time-equivalent research and development scientists and engineers in the industry workforce (5.9 percent). I refer to this innovation-based definition of industries as "technology generators" because they are generators of technology, even though they may not employ a large number of technology-related occupations. Appendix A shows a list of the NAICS industries that are technology generators in comparison to technology employers.[1] It is important to note that the second component of this definition also relies on science and technical workforce concentration. However, these are only research and development related positions; thus, some technology generator industries are essentially a subset of technology employers, with two exceptions. Technology generators have only two industries that are not included in the technology employers' list: plastics and resin manufacturing and synthetic rubber manufacturing. On the other side, the technology generators list does not include thirty of the industries included on the technology employers' list, including defense-related industries, machinery manufacturing, and pharmaceuticals. The examples of technology employer industries provided above are drawn from these thirty industries.

The two sectoral definitions offered here, technology employers and technology generators, offer the advantage of including both of the elements considered vital to technology-driven economic growth—human capital and innovative capacity. In addition, both the human capital and innovation definitions also provide linkages to present and future local economic development and growth in the technology economy.

The Technology Economy and Local Governments

The previous sections provided an overview of the technology economy and it components. Transparent definitions and discussion of both the infrastructure and the sectors of the technology economy are important if we are to better understand how the technology economy affects economic development policy. This book seeks to provide a local analysis of both the infrastructure and the sectors, enabling a more complete understanding of what the possibilities are for policymakers, and in addition, an understanding of what localities can do and are doing about deploying technology economy infrastructure and attracting and retaining technology economy industry.

The current focus of much of the analysis in this arena is on how regions are faring and adapting to a service-based, globalizing, and technological economy (Florida 2005a, 2002; Barnes and Ledebur 1998; Saxenian 1996; Chapple et al. 2004; Cortright and Mayer 2001). Although regions make sense in terms of an economic unit of analysis, they are far less tractable as a political unit of analysis. Virtually no regional governments exist that have equivalent powers and authorities to those found at the state or local government level. Even though local governments are a creation of state charters, they are the political and administrative units that govern a range of political and social activities. Local governments are comprised of mayors, city council members, commissioners, and aldermen who are elected to represent the interests of local citizens (Glasson 1978; Pickvance 1990; Wong 2002). These local officials make decisions about economic development strategies and local needs. Cities engage in economic development because they want to increase revenue stability, decrease external shocks, provide good jobs, and increase the overall satisfaction of city residents (Clarke and Gaile 1998; Peterson 1981). These political and administrative powers are the key as to why it is essential to assess how the infrastructure and sectors of the technology economy affect localities and what actions they are taking to manipulate the outcomes. Although many stress the importance of regions and states, focusing on these units exhibits a vast incompatibility between economic development practice and the political partitioning of space (Beauregard 1993). The nation's economic regions are governed by loosely attached networks of local political units and their representatives; they are therefore the most appropriate and realistic unit of analysis.

Cities seek to be part of the technology economy by attracting, retaining, and growing technology economy industries. Deploying technology economy infrastructure is seen as one way to make a place more attractive to these industries. Technology economy industries are just as likely to need this infrastructure as any other business, if not more so. Regardless of whether cities are targeting technology economy industries, there is still a need for investment in technology economy infrastructure as a means of providing local services and attracting other industries that are less reliant upon this infrastructure, but still use it and deem it to be a valuable component in their operations. A variety of questions thus emerge for city officials: Is the city's technology economy infrastructure adequate or lacking, and regardless, what communities in the city are at a disadvantage—where are the dead zones? The city's capacity to provide technology economy infrastructure—whether independently or through partnerships—is an extremely important part of operating in the technology economy.

Issues in Technology Economy Research at the City Level

This book examines the intersection of local governments and the technology economy in terms of economic development policy choices and strategies involved with technology infrastructure and sectors. Two key challenges to this type of analysis are access to and availability of data, and an analytic, or scholarly, debate about whether local governments are the appropriate unit of analysis.

The first challenge is a data problem. Technology economy data, infrastructure and sectoral, are usually lumped together and lack the necessary distinctions to separate the various components, confusing analyses about how to measure the technology economy's impacts and how localities can harness technology economy growth. In defining both of the infrastructure and sectoral building blocks, and the relationship between the two pieces, it is necessary to separate the benefits from infrastructure and sectors. In previous work, I have examined the question of how the infrastructure of the technology economy influences sectoral growth, and whether the infrastructure is consequential to the technology economy's sectoral growth (Hackler 2003a, 2004, 2003b). This question presents a chicken-and-egg problem—does the infrastructure need to exist before the industries will locate in a jurisdiction, or is a sound industrial base of these industries needed before private and public infrastructure investors will develop and deploy the infrastructure? Little research has been conducted to clarify the relationship between infrastructure and sectors. Partially, this is because the infrastructure side of the technology economy is harder to analyze, primarily due to the lack of data on existing infrastructure at a disaggregated, or local, level. Most of the technology infrastructure data, as defined here, is proprietary data and in the hands of private sector telecommunications companies. Although these companies report to the Federal Communications Commission, in the case of fiber-optic fiber, the companies are only required to report at the telephone area code level. These aggregate data are difficult to use because area codes simply do not match city jurisdictions, or for that matter regional or state boundaries. For example, the state of Idaho has only one area code, but the Los Angeles metropolitan area has as many as eleven area codes, and there are complex and sometimes vague descriptions of the coverage area, such as the 323 area code often being described as the "doughnut" around the core of downtown Los Angeles, including communities like Bell, Cudahy, Huntington Park, Hyde Park, Silver Lake, Vernon, Watts, most of Hollywood, Montebello, and South Gate, and parts of Alhambra, Beverly Hills, Commerce, Inglewood, Los Angeles, Monterey Park, Pasadena, and West Hollywood. Unclear geographical assignment and the fact that a city may have multiple telecommunications providers mixed in with its own infrastructure makes data collection at the local level more arduous. A number of private geographical mapping firms claim to have a number of the infrastructure components available for sale, but the barriers of price and questionable accuracy cast a shadow on these options.

In comparison to the availability of infrastructure data, the national economic census provides a wealth of data on the sectoral front, including establishments, employees, and payroll. The availability of these data is probably the most likely reason why much of the analysis of the technology economy concentrates on economic sectors.

Despite the lack of availability of local infrastructure data, analysis of the infrastructure remains important because of the connection between the infrastructure and the sectors of the technology economy. This book presents new infrastructure data, based on a survey of cities conducted in 2002, the Economic Development and Technology Economy Survey. The survey was conducted in an attempt to understand what cities have in place in terms of technology economy infrastructure. Chapters 3 and 4 describe this survey in greater depth and utilize the data to examine the technology economy in cities.

Beyond data challenges, an additional debate exists about whether local governments are the appropriate unit of analysis. Most of the research on the technology economy components has not been conducted at the local level. The sectoral analyses focus on national, state, and regional, or metropolitan economies. The regional- and metropolitan-level analyses are the closest to the local level. Florida (2002), Barnes and Ledebur (1998), and others argue that this is appropriate because regions are the subelements of our national economy. Data collection at the regional level is also easier. Research on agglomeration economies—the idea that spillover benefits accrue because a business is either close to similar businesses or close to a diversity of suppliers and workforce options—also points to regional-level analysis as being appropriate and acceptable. However, if we assume that economic growth is not all due to exogenous factors, that is to say that some endogenous factors and actions can influence an economy's direction, then regional-level analyses lack an important input—the actions and policies of corresponding political and administrative units. In endogenous growth models, government policies and actions can influence the long-run growth rate because many policies affect the level of innovation in the economy (Romer 1986; Lucas 1988). Also, in the United States there are few regional governments that possess the responsibility and capacity to influence regional growth; it is only at the local government level that both policy and institutional mechanisms of government exist for addressing the regional economy—budgeting, taxation, provision of infrastructure, regulations, and maintenance of law and order. The local level, and city government in particular, is the unit of analysis most appropriate for analyzing the relationship between the technology economy's infrastructure, sectoral growth, and policymaking.

To analyze the technology economy sectors at the local level, this book uses data available from the Census Bureau's Business Register.[2] However, instead of using metropolitan area or county statistics to create the technology sectors, I use the most disaggregated data available. The Census Bureau reports these data at the ZIP code level by six-digit NAICS codes that, with some manipulation, become suitable for city-level analysis (U.S. Census Bureau 2001b).[3] Chapter 3 presents the technology sector analysis.

Cities and Technology
Economy Sectors

Since the early 1980s, economy watchers have been struck by the dynamism of new industries, dubbed high tech, and their apparent roles in driving differential regional growth rates. Older industrial and financial cities, such as New York and Chicago, which were growing slowly and were subject to considerable deindustrialization, no longer seemed capable of performing as "seedbeds of innovation," whereas such places as Silicon Valley and Route 128 outside Boston became famous as prototype new industrial regions.

—*Karen Chapple, Ann Markusen, Greg Schrock,*
Daisaku Yamamoto, and Pingkang Yu

What are the characteristics of cities that are succeeding in the technology economy? How do these cities compare to cities not performing as well? This chapter examines the relationship between cities and employment in technology economy sectors in order to provide a perspective on which cities are leading and lagging in the technology sectors, the economic and demographic characteristics of these cities, and their technology infrastructure.

The research presented in this chapter analyzes secondary data on employment for the 252 cities that responded to the Economic Development and Technology Economy Survey, a nationwide survey of economic development officials in cities conducted from June through August of 2002. The survey represents the first data collection of telecommunications infrastructure attempted at the local level for a large comparative sample. The survey focused on economic development and the role of the technology economy in the local economy as a strategy for economic development. Local officials were queried on economic conditions, current economic development policies and business attraction plans, existing telecommunications infrastructure attributes (including improvements and private-public partnerships), the role of telecommunications in economic development activities, and finally, a number of local government characteristics. The results of the survey are presented in Chapter 4.[1] However, this chapter matches the national employment data, collected for the technology economy sectors defined in Chapter 2, to the 252 cities that responded to the Economic Development and Technology Economy Survey. The sector data are drawn from Zip Code Business Patterns (similar to County Business Patterns and extracted from the same data sources), collected as part of the Business Register of the U.S. Census Bureau (U.S. Census Bureau 2001a, 2001b, 1997).[2] The ZIP code–level data enable analysis for geographical areas below the county level on a yearly basis. The Zip Code Business Patterns data used here include counts of employment and establishments[3] by ZIP code and six-digit NAICS codes for the entire United States for 2001 (U.S. Census Bureau 2001b). As explained in Chapter 2, I manipulated the ZIP code data and aggregated them by city to create measures of total employment and establishments for each city, and I did the same for the technology economy sectors—technology employers and technology generators.[4] In addition, I collected other city-level data from sources like the Census of Population and Housing for 2000 and County and City Data Book 2000 to supplement the survey as well as assess the accuracy and validity of the local government responses on general economic characteristics (U.S. Census Bureau 2000a and 2000b). The collection of additional data from secondary sources enhances the level of comparison for this representative sample of local governments. The following section explores this sample relative to how cities are performing in the technology economy in terms of technology sectors and other city characteristics.

Leading and Lagging Cities in Technology Economy Sectors

The technology economy relies heavily on human capital and innovation, both as inputs and outputs, in order to generate future economic development; consequently, I capture the effect of these two components in the technology sector definitions discussed in Chapter 2. Technology employers are those industries that have three times the national average employment of people in scientific and technical occupations. Technology generators are closely related, but more tied to technology economy research and development. Technology generator industries have above-average investment in research and development and above-average employment in scientific and engineering occupations that focus on research and development. Both technology sectors include the industries that have innovative potential, which is an important concern of local economic development practitioners wishing to grow resilient industries that are more likely to create spin-off businesses and weather the product cycle more gracefully. Also important is that the industries included in both technology sectors have great workforce similarities, providing what are generally considered to be higher-skill, higher-wage jobs. A city with a diverse base of these industries may also be better off in times of recession or expansion because the bulk of these industries' workforces are complementary (Chapple et al. 2004).

To explore what types of cities are more likely to be home to businesses in these technology sectors, I rank the cities in the survey by the percentage of employment in the technology employer and technology generator sectors. This creates two ratios, one for a city's employment in technology employer industries divided by total employment in all industries, and the other for technology generator industries. The average employment for technology employers was 4.17 percent; however, the cities ranged from 0.19 to 36.34 percent. For technology generators, the average city employment was only 2.83 percent,[5] and the range was slightly smaller, from no employment in the sector to 32.61 percent. However, there is less variation across cities in terms of employment in the technology employer sector than for technology generators, with a coefficient of variation[6] of 0.84 compared to 1.05. Employment for technology employers is more consistent across the cities in the sample.

The rankings of the top ten cities in terms of employment in the two technology sectors demonstrate the effect that the technology economy has on these cities (see Table 3.1). For both sectors, at least one out of every ten workers in the analyzed cities is an employee of a technology establishment, ranging from 11.21 to 36.64 percent of a city's employment. Nine of the cities perform well in both sectors. As discussed in Chapter 2, some overlap of industries occurs for these two technology sectors. The cities performing well in technology employer and technology generator industries are in regions of the United States associated with technology industries. Four of the top ten cities are located in or around the Silicon Valley in California (Sunnyvale, Alameda, San Jose, and San Mateo). Ridgecrest, California, is in the Mojave Desert but is right next to the China Lake Naval Weapons Center. Cary, North

Table 3.1

Leading and Lagging Cities for Technology Employers and Technology Generators by Percent Employment (%) and Location Quotient (LQ), 2001 (N = 252)

	Technology employers	%	LQ	Technology generators	%	LQ
				Leading cities		
1	Sunnyvale, CA	36.64	6.46	Sunnyvale, CA	32.61	8.37
2	Ridgecrest, CA	18.43	3.25	Ridgecrest, CA	16.46	4.23
3	Alameda, CA	17.27	3.04	Alameda, CA	15.05	3.86
4	San Jose, CA	16.43	2.90	San Jose, CA	14.05	3.61
5	San Mateo, CA	15.91	2.80	Camarillo, CA	12.62	3.24
6	Cary, NC	14.83	2.61	Cary, NC	12.38	3.18
7	Bellevue, WA	14.78	2.60	Bellevue, WA	11.65	2.99
8	Camarillo, CA	14.14	2.49	Hampton, VA	11.30	2.90
9	Ann Arbor, MI	13.53	2.39	Ann Arbor, MI	11.30	2.90
10	San Diego, CA	12.81	2.26	San Mateo, CA	11.21	2.88
				Lagging cities		
1	Athens, TN	.19	.03	Mexico, MO	.00	.00
2	Loma Linda, CA	.21	.04	Lancaster, TX	.03	.01
3	Atchison, KS	.25	.04	Loma Linda, CA	.04	.01
4	Lancaster, TX	.31	.05	Casa Grande, AZ	.05	.01
5	Montebello, CA	.31	.05	Montebello, CA	.06	.02
6	Farmington, MO	.32	.06	Parsons, KS	.07	.02
7	Chillicothe, OH	.39	.07	Athens, TN	.09	.02
8	Maple Heights, OH	.40	.07	Centralia, IL	.15	.04
9	Centralia, IL	.42	.07	Passaic, NJ	.19	.05
10	The Dalles, OR	.52	.09	Hempstead, NY	.20	.05

Source: ZIP Code Business Patterns (U.S. Census Bureau 2001b).

Carolina, is part of the Research Triangle regional economy in the Raleigh-Durham area. Bellevue, Washington, is east of Seattle but within ten miles of Redmond, home of the Microsoft Corporation. Ann Arbor, Michigan, is home to one of the nation's premier research universities, the University of Michigan. Two cities appear in the top ten of one sector but not in both sector rankings. San Diego appears on the technology employer list while Hampton, Virginia, located near the Norfolk Naval Base, is eighth on the technology generator list.

The rankings by percent employment in each of the technology sectors for these ten cities are equivalent to the ranking by location quotients. Location quotients are commonly used in comparisons of economic bases because they compare city or regional performance to the national performance; that is, the location quotient is the ratio of local technology employer or generator employment to local total employment divided by the ratio of the nation's technology employer or generator employment to national total employment for 2001. When the location quotient is equal to one, the city's share of employment in the sector is equal to the national share of employment in the same sector. However, when the location quotient is greater than one, the local employment shares are larger than the national shares of employment in the sector, indicating a greater-than-average concentration of such employment. The location quotient estimate reveals that local production in a sector is specialized. The interpretation of location quotients provides further context to employment percentages. For the rankings in Table 3.1, over one-third (36.64 percent) of employees working in establishments in Sunnyvale, California, the heart of the Silicon Valley, are working in industries that are defined as technology employers. This seems to be a very high percentage, and the location quotient corroborates the finding. Sunnyvale has almost twice the share of technology employment in both technology employer and technology generator industries of Ridgecrest, California, the second city in the top ten on both lists.

Cities not performing as well in technology economy employment are not as regionally clustered as many of the top ten cities. Again, there is some overlap of cities in the bottom ten on both of the rankings based on percent employment and location quotients for technology employers and generators. The comparison of the cities leading in technology economy employment with those lagging behind indicates wide disparities. Even the best-performing city of the lagging group has less than one-half of a percent employment in the technology economy sectors. The location quotients for this group indicate that none of these cities is even close to having a share of technology employment equal to that of the national economy. One of the most interesting results of this comparison is that the cities lagging in the technology economy sectors are relatively dispersed, favoring no one region, unlike the cities in the top ten. In addition, none of the lagging cities is located near or in any of the regions that include the cities in the top ten on either of the lists. The technology economy is often purported to show a regional preference, agglomerating in regions like the Silicon Valley (Bresnahan and Gambardella 2004; Saxenian 1996). The results of this analysis of sector data for the surveyed cities support this claim.

An additional point of interest is the type of city that is leading or lagging in the technology economy sectors. For technology employers, only two cities, both leaders, have populations among the largest in the United States. San Diego ranked seventh and San Jose eleventh by population among cities nationwide in 2003.[7] Yet none of the cities on either the leading or lagging rankings for technology generators is large. This is not an artifact of the sample of cities responding to the survey. In fact, the surveyed respondents include 6 of the top 11 cities ranked by population nationally in 2000 (New York, Los Angeles, Chicago, San Diego, Dallas, and San Jose), and 23 of the top 50. Consequently, the technology sector rankings suggest that large cities may not necessarily possess an advantage in technology sectors. Larger cities are more likely to have a greater diversity of industries than smaller ones, which may indicate that technology economy sectors are less likely to lead in large cities.[8] In addition, of the two large cities appearing in the rankings, San Jose's growth is tied to the Silicon Valley's growth, drawing 14.4 percent population growth during the 1990s when the technology economy was booming. Finally, the comparison of technology employer and generator sectors in cities shows what many unidimensional sector definitions cannot— the relationship between innovation and human capital industries, apparent even at the local level. The similarities and differences in the rankings convey more insight into a city's relative advantage in human capital or innovation industries vis-à-vis other cities. This knowledge has potential when cities are crafting policies that can accentuate their advantages while addressing their weaknesses.

Technology Economy Subsectors

The analysis of the leading and lagging cities also shows some variation in the location of technology sectors. As noted, two cities (San Diego and Hampton, VA) appear in the top ten of one sector but not in both sector rankings. The definitions of technology employers and technology generators are based on human capital and innovation measures; however, there are similarities among these industries for each sector. To highlight the interrelationships among sectors that aggregate analysis cannot, I separate the industries into product-related subsectors. For the technology employers, I identify six subsectors: (1) chemicals, petroleum, and pharmaceuticals; (2) defense-related; (3) hardware and communications equipment; (4) manufacturing, machinery, and instruments; (5) services research and development; and (6) software and Internet services. The subsectors for technology generators are similar but differ due to the definition used to select technology generator industries. Some industries included in the technology employer subsectors are not industries that have greater-than-average research and development expenditures, and thus are not defined as technology generators. There are only five subsectors for technology generators: (1) chemicals and petroleum; (2) hardware and communications equipment; (3) manufacturing instruments; (4) services research and development; and (5) software. The subsectors more clearly identify the differences in industries discussed in Chapter 2. In the chemicals and petroleum subsector of technology generators, pharmaceutical industries are not included. No defense-related industries are selected as technology generators using the criteria described in Chapter 2, such as aerospace and aircraft manufacturing or missile and space vehicle parts; consequently, there is no defense-related subsector for the technology generators sector. The hardware and communications equipment subsector for technology generators does not include audio and video equipment manufacturing. The manufacturing instruments subsector for technology generators does not include any machine manufacturing industries that were selected as technology employers. The technology generators subsector for services research and development does not include either management, scientific, and technical consulting services, or professional and commercial equipment wholesalers (office, computer, and computer peripheral equipment and medical equipment) industries. Finally, the software subsector for technology generators does not include Internet-related services. Again, each of these subsector differences is because some of the industries selected as being technology employers do not have above-average research and development expenditures as technology generator industries must have.

The subsector rankings for the top ten cities by percentage of city employment in each subsector help to explain some of the differences between sectors (see Tables 3.2 and 3.3). San Diego slips in as the tenth leading city for technology employers because 8.37 percent of the city's employment is in the services research and development industries, placing the city in eleventh place for that subsector. Hampton ranks eighth among the top ten cities with employment in industries defined as technology generators, in part because it ranks fifth, with 9.34 percent of the city's employment in services research and development industries. It is also interesting to note that cities like Mexico, Missouri, and Parsons,

Table 3.2

Leading Cities in Subsectors of Technology Employers by Percent Employment, 2001 (N = 252)

Leading cities

	Chemicals Petro Pharm		Defense-related	
1	Niagara Falls, NY	3.73	Kerrville, TX	2.81
2	Kankakee, IL	3.19	Manchester, CT	2.39
3	Old Bridge, NJ	2.84	Parsons, KS	2.33
4	Worthington, MN	2.64	Monrovia, CA	1.84
5	Port Arthur, TX	2.31	Garden Grove, CA	1.76
6	Mexico, MO	2.18	Pinellas Park, FL	1.72
7	Chicago Heights, IL	1.91	San Marcos, TX	1.49
8	Garden Grove, CA	1.73	Wichita, KS	1.27
9	Ogden, UT	1.60	West Haven, CT	1.19
10	Vacaville, CA	1.55	Hanford, CA	.96
	Hardware Comm Eqp		**Mfg Machine Instruments**	
1	Sunnyvale, CA	9.87	Westwood, MA	4.39
2	Camarillo, CA	7.99	Sunnyvale, CA	3.94
3	San Jose, CA	4.92	Solon, OH	3.24
4	Lowell, MA	4.83	Grants Pass, OR	3.09
5	Lebanon, IN	4.73	Monrovia, CA	3.00
6	Springboro, OH	4.34	De Land, FL	2.93
7	Old Bridge, NJ	3.54	Palm Bay, FL	2.82
8	Minnetonka, MN	3.38	Concord, NH	2.51
9	Franklin, WI	3.19	San Jose, CA	2.30
10	Morgan Hill, CA	3.09	Pinellas Park, FL	2.22
	Services R&D		**Software and Internet Services**	
1	Sunnyvale, CA	18.06	San Mateo, CA	5.89
2	Ridgecrest, CA	17.79	Sunnyvale, CA	4.56
3	Alameda, CA	12.87	Mansfield, MA	4.44
4	Cary, NC	11.68	Bellevue, WA	3.79
5	Ann Arbor, MI	10.53	Morgan Hill, CA	2.91
6	Bellevue, WA	10.38	Santa Monica, CA	2.89
7	Hampton, VA	9.65	Pleasanton, CA	2.86
8	San Mateo, CA	9.22	Westwood, MA	2.76
9	Troy, MI	9.00	Troy, MI	2.68
10	San Carlos, CA	8.41	Lombard, IL	2.62

Source: ZIP Code Business Patterns (U.S. Census Bureau 2001b).
Note: Petro pharm = petrochemicals and pharmaceuticals; Comm eqp = communications equipment; Mfg = manufacturing; R&D = research and development.

Kansas, are in the top ten of two technology employer subsectors—the chemicals, petroleum, and pharmaceuticals, and defense-related subsectors, respectively; however, both cities are lagging in the technology generator sector, ranked in the bottom ten cities. These two cities

Table 3.3

Leading Cities in Subsectors of Technology Generators by Percent Employment, 2001 (*N* = 252)

	Leading cities			
	Chemicals and Petro			
1	Orange, TX	10.12		
2	Niagara Falls, NY	3.76		
3	Port Arthur, TX	3.15		
4	Old Bridge, NJ	2.84		
5	Chicago Heights, IL	2.09		
6	Marshall, TX	1.32		
7	Garfield Heights, OH	1.07		
8	Urbana, IL	.95		
9	Baton Rouge, LA	.89		
10	Joliet, IL	.80		
	Hardware Comm Eqp		**Mfg Instruments**	
1	Sunnyvale, CA	9.88	Westwood, MA	4.50
2	Camarillo, CA	7.63	Grants Pass, OR	3.08
3	San Jose, CA	4.91	De Land, FL	2.89
4	Lowell, MA	4.87	Sunnyvale, CA	2.64
5	Lebanon, IN	4.73	Monrovia, CA	1.93
6	Old Bridge, NJ	3.54	Solon, OH	1.83
7	Minnetonka, MN	3.38	San Jose, CA	1.44
8	Franklin, WI	3.20	Broken Arrow, OK	1.16
9	Morgan Hill, CA	3.15	Laramie, WY	1.16
10	Logansport, IN	3.07	Santa Cruz, CA	1.05
	Services R&D		**Software**	
1	Sunnyvale, CA	17.28	San Mateo, CA	2.99
2	Ridgecrest, CA	16.06	Sunnyvale, CA	2.81
3	Alameda, CA	11.47	Bellevue, WA	2.24
4	Cary, NC	10.11	La Palma, CA	2.13
5	Hampton, VA	9.34	Alameda, CA	2.08
6	Ann Arbor, MI	9.06	Santa Cruz, CA	1.86
7	Bellevue, WA	9.03	Evanston, IL	1.85
8	Troy, MI	7.98	Santa Monica, CA	1.79
9	San Mateo, CA	7.65	Pleasanton, CA	1.70
10	San Diego, CA	7.34	Cary, NC	1.62

Source: ZIP Code Business Patterns (U.S. Census Bureau 2001b).

Note: Petro = petrochemicals; Comm eqp = communications equipment; Mfg = manufacturing; R&D = research and development.

demonstrate that there are important distinctions among sets of industries in the technology economy—whether they are more strongly based in human capital or innovation. However, the differences would not be apparent without examining the subsectors of each technology sector.

Monolithic analysis of industries does not reveal enough variation, and this is especially true when examining local economies. A city might not have a concentration across many industries in the technology sectors, but it might have a concentration in a few industries. Analysis of the subsectors enables a level of data disaggregation that is useful in examining geographical location tendencies of technology economy industries and hints at which cities are better locations for human capital and innovation industries.

Technology Employer Subsectors

Turning to the rankings of cities in the sectors and subsectors of technology employers, all cities except San Diego appear in the top ten of at least one of the technology employer subsectors (Table 3.2). Hardware communications equipment, manufacturing machine instruments, services research and development, and software and Internet services have large presences in Sunnyvale. However, cities like Ridgecrest, Alameda, and Camarillo, California, Cary, North Carolina, and Ann Arbor, Michigan, appear in the top ten of just one subsector. Only the Silicon Valley cities in California and the city of Bellevue, Washington, seem to have a presence in multiple subsectors. The "tech" reputations of the regions to which these cities belong are definitely apparent, but the cities in the region also show the diversity of industries that are located in the cities and their regions. At the other end the spectrum, two subsectors of technology employers include cities that are not ranked for the entire technology employers sector. In fact, for chemicals, petroleum, and pharmaceuticals, and defense-related subsectors, the top ten cities are not even located in regions traditionally reputed as being technology havens. Half of the leaders in the chemicals, petroleum, and pharmaceuticals subsector are in the Northeast or Midwest. With respect to the defense-related subsector, four states have more than one city leading the subsector—Texas, Connecticut, Kansas, and California—and most of the cities fit the traditional description of suburbs. This observation is not completely unexpected, as Peter Dreier, John Mollenkopf, and Todd Swanstrom argue (2002). According to them, military spending was effectively the nation's industrial policy, and its expenditures—military facilities and wartime production facilities—were largely concentrated in suburban locations. The remaining subsectors have a mix of sector-leading cities and nonleaders, as in the hardware and communications equipment and manufacturing, machine, and instruments subsectors. However, the remaining two technology employer subsectors have multiple technology employer leaders, especially the services research and development subsector. It is this subsector that also accounts for the largest portions of city employment in the technology employers sector, with six of the top ten cities having one out of every ten workers employed in services research and development. Moreover, Sunnyvale and Ridgecrest are close to having one employee out of every five in the services research and development subsector. The movement in the U.S. economy from a manufacturing to a service base is quite apparent in the employment of this subsector as well as the software and Internet services subsector.

Technology Generator Subsectors

In contrast, the technology generator subsectors present a less diverse set of cities; the research and development criterion seems to create subsector rankings more similar to the overall sector ranking than found in the technology employer rankings (Table 3.3). Sunnyvale continues to dominate four of the five technology generator subsectors: hardware and communications equipment, manufacturing instruments, services research and development, and software, and cities like Ridgecrest and Camarillo, California, Hampton, Virginia, and Ann Arbor, Michigan, appear in the top ten of given subsectors. As with the technology employer subsectors, the Silicon Valley cities and Bellevue, Washington, have a presence in multiple subsectors, as does Cary, North Carolina, a Research Triangle area city; this further exhibits the technology economy reputations of these regions.

The leaders of technology generators appear on all rankings except for the chemicals and petroleum subsector, where half of the leaders are in the Northeast or Midwest. Three Texas cities also dominate the list, and two, Port Arthur and Orange, are within forty miles of each other. The city ranking for the hardware and communications equipment subsector is similar to the technology employer ranking because the innovation definition excluded only one industry. Thus, the exchange of Springboro, Ohio, for Logansport, Indiana, is due to the exclusion of the audio and video equipment industry. Outside of the four California cities, the subsector has a significant presence in the Midwest and Northeast. The changes in the ranking for the manufacturing and instruments subsector are a result of the exclusion of the machinery manufacturing industries. Sunnyvale falls down in the list while San Jose rises, and the percentage of employment for all cities in this sector, except Westwood, Massachusetts, is less for technology generators as compared to technology employers. The services research and development subsector excludes management and technical consulting and professional equipment wholesalers, thus the ranking demonstrates only cities that are stronger in engineering, physical and life sciences, and testing services. Even with this change, the set of leading cities for this subsector is similar to that in the technology employer subsector for services research and development, except San Diego, which is ranked here due to its concentration in the engineering and physical and life scientific services. This subsector also accounts for the largest portions of city employment in the technology generator sector, with four of the top ten cities having one out of every ten workers employed in services research and development. Finally, the software subsector ranking is interesting in comparison to that for the technology employers because of the exclusion of Internet services industries. Cities such as Mansfield and Westwood, Massachusetts, Morgan Hill, California, Troy, Michigan, and Lombard, Illinois, made the top ten for software and Internet services for the technology employers sector, mostly due to their employment in the Internet services industries. When these industries are excluded to meet the technology generator criteria, La Palma, Alameda, and Santa Cruz, California, along with Evanston, Illinois, and Cary, North Carolina, move onto the list. The comparison of the subsectors for both technology employers and generators reveals greater variation and specialization among local economies and their presences in the technology economy.

City Characteristics and Technology Sectors

The analysis of the leading and lagging cities in the technology sectors reveals a number of patterns with regard to regional agglomeration of industries as well as subsector differences in the locations of technology economy industries. Although the rankings allow for a comparison of the leading and lagging cities and among the leaders of the subsectors, they do not characterize the cities that are performing well or poorly in the technology economy. The following analysis focuses on comparisons of traditional social and economic characteristics as well as technology infrastructure in the surveyed cities and relates these to their employment in the technology sectors. For Tables 3.4, 3.5, and 3.6, I place cities in four groups (quartiles) based on their employment in the technology sectors, grouped from lowest employment (1st quartile) to highest employment (4th quartile)[9] and calculate the appropriate measure of central tendency for each of the socioeconomic characteristics for each group of cities. This allows a systematic comparison of characteristics among cities in the lower quartiles of employment to those in the higher quartiles. The tables include the comparison of characteristics by quartile for both sectors as well as the appropriate measure of central tendency for the entire sample.[10]

Technology Sectors and Economic Characteristics

The first comparison (Table 3.4) relates to the economic climates of the cities with technology economy employment. Cities with greater employment in technology employer industries have significantly different and greater total employment growth (1998 to 2001). However, for cities with greater employment in technology generator industries, the second quartile has higher average employment growth than the fourth, indicating that technology generators seem to be located in cities with greater concentrations, but not those at the most concentrated level.[11] Cities with greater technology employer sector employment have less unemployment overall. The remaining measures have similar comparisons for the two sectors. A measure strongly associated with innovation is the number of patents. Although not a perfect measure, a patent indicates that the inventor's research met a threshold for innovative activity.[12] Industries with greater research and development expenditures and the scientific and engineering workforce to utilize these expenditures should be correlated with greater patent production. Here, I measure patents as a sum of all granted patents for inventors in a city from 1991 to 1999 relative to that city's population; this shows the innovative capacity of the city during the decade preceding employment in the two sectors.[13] As expected, cities generating more patents relative to population do have greater employment in both technology sectors. In fact, the fourth quartiles of both sectors—those with the highest levels of employment—have almost two times the number of patents relative to population than the third quartiles, showing higher levels of concentration of innovation in cities with higher technology economy employment. The remaining economic characteristics relate to income and cost of living.

Table 3.4

Technology Employers and Generators Employment by Economic Characteristics

	Technology Employers				
	Mean/Mode	Quartile 1	Quartile 2	Quartile 3	Quartile 4
Employment growth rate (%)	7.55**	4.20	5.92	11.52	10.70
Patents per 1,000 pop.	3.14***	1.45	2.12	2.94	7.64
Unemployment rate (%)	4.74***	5.79	4.70	3.97	3.84
Per capita income	24,070**	22,470	21,730	25,630	28,900
Median household income	43,600***	35,822	39,019	46,028	60,147
% Poverty	12.14***	14.46	14.09	10.46	7.61
Housing affordability rate	0.46***	0.50	0.50	0.43	0.38

	Technology Generators				
	Mean/Mode	Quartile 1	Quartile 2	Quartile 3	Quartile 4
Employment growth rate (%)	7.56*	5.06	6.99	12.23	6.19
Patents per 1,000 pop.	3.14***	1.24	1.90	3.23	6.12
Unemployment rate (%)	4.74***	5.79	4.64	4.06	4.37
Per capita income	24,070***	21,050	24,230	25,310	26,120
Median household income	43,601***	35,099	40,789	45,817	52,578
% Poverty	12.14***	15.13	12.52	11.28	9.66
Housing affordability rate	0.46***	0.53	0.47	0.45	0.40

Sources: Employment (U.S. Census Bureau 2001b); patents (Hall, Jaffe, and Trajtenberg 2001); unemployment, incomes, poverty, and housing affordability rate (ratio of median family income to median value of owner-occupied housing) (U.S. Census Bureau 2000a).

Note: Significance levels = *** at 0.01, ** at 0.05, and * at 0.10.

Cities with greater technology employer and generator employment have higher per capita and median household incomes and fewer people living in poverty. However, housing is less affordable in cities with greater technology economy employment. These cities are growing economically, and growth puts price pressures on all inputs and factors, especially the cost of living, as more people move into these areas to take advantage of the economic climates. Overall, the analysis reveals that cities with greater technology employment are also faring well economically. The relationship between the technology economy and economic growth is clear; however, we are not sure whether the economy is doing well because of the technology sectors or whether the technology sectors are doing well because of the economy. Statistical analysis in the sections to follow will more closely examine this relationship.

Technology Sectors and Demographics

With indications that the technology economy is positively related to economic growth in cities, understanding how the technology sectors relate to other city demographics is key in providing more context to this phenomenon (Table 3.5). The populations of cities performing well in technology employer and generator industries are larger and younger, with more people 25 to 34 years of age and considerably fewer people over the age of 64. Florida (2002) points to a younger demographic in his work examining the creative class as a driving force of economic growth. The youthful energy, mobility, and fewer family commitments of this demographic group give them the potential to be more innovative and creative (less averse to risk), which can reverberate through the companies in which they work and the local economies in which they live. The age factors are related to educational demographics; cities with greater technology sector employment also have significantly higher percentages of college graduates. Level of education and number of years of school are prime measures of human capital, and the accrual of human capital is measured in the technology sector definitions as being comprised of occupations that require at least a college education, if not more. An educated labor pool, as noted in other studies, continues to be a favored location factor for technology sector companies (Florida 2002; Chapple et al. 2004; Hackler 2003a, 2004; Markusen, Hall, and Glasmeier 1986; Malecki 1991, 1997).

The incidence of violent crimes is slightly higher in cities with greater

Table 3.5

Technology Employers and Generators Employment by Social Demographics

		Technology employers			
	Mean/Mode	Quartile 1	Quartile 2	Quartile 3	Quartile 4
Population 2000	62,830	30,765	62,673	66,846	113,968
% College graduates	16.28***	12.48	13.65	17.76	24.51
% Black	9.87**	10.13	13.68	8.91	5.62
% Age 25–34	10.55	10.28	10.62	10.42	11.11
% Over age 64	13.31***	14.53	12.84	13.94	11.03
% Violent crime rate	9.96	9.16	9.22	11.25	10.37

		Technology generators			
	Mean/Mode	Quartile 1	Quartile 2	Quartile 3	Quartile 4
Population 2000	62,830	26,409	43,765	85,188	96,354
% College graduates	16.28***	11.65	14.8	17.22	21.38
% Black	9.87	10.92	11.01	7.99	9.46
% Age 25–34	10.55*	10.40	10.24	10.47	11.10
% Over age 64	13.31	14.19	13.77	12.50	12.77
% Violent crime rate	11.06	11.67	9.29	11.63	11.66

Sources: Population, college graduates, race, and age categories (U.S. Census Bureau 2000a); crime (U.S. Federal Bureau of Investigation 1999).

Note: Significance levels = *** at 0.01, ** at 0.05, and * at 0.10.

technology employment. But in examining all quartile means, the levels are not significantly different, and they are not consistently increasing or decreasing across the quartiles. Crime, unfortunately, is part of any city. In terms of its effect on business development, recent research by Robert Greenbaum and George Tita shows that violence has a varied effect on different types of businesses. They find that violence has the greatest effect on services-related (retail and personal) business, but such industries are not defined as technology economy sectors (Greenbaum and Tita 2004).

The final demographic measure in Table 3.5 points to a more troubling issue. Cities with greater technology employer employment have a smaller black population; this relationship is not as consistent in cities with greater technology generator employment, where the first, second, and fourth quartiles are similar to the first quartile of the technology employer employment. However, for industries in which scientific and engineering occupations are three times the national average, there seems to be a strong indication that they are not located in cities with larger populations of people of color. Florida produced similar results in his analysis of high-technology industries and diversity—black, and other nonwhite populations (Florida 2002). The relative lack of quality education and training opportunities found among populations of people of color are likely factors contributing to these aggregate findings. The results suggest that cities may need to address such disconnects and examine how the schools, other education programs, and industry-based training programs could create a niche in the technology economy.

Technology Sectors and Location

The analysis of demographic characteristics suggests that certain cities are more likely to have technology industries. The profile of a city that enjoys greater employment in the technology sectors describes a population that is youthful, better educated, and likely to be larger, yet the type of location is not as divergent. In addition to regions of the United States, I examined three location classifications for the sample cities: whether they are designated as urban or rural,[14] a metropolitan or micropolitan statistical area,[15] and a principal city of these areas or not (see Table 3.6). Regardless of the percentage of technology employer employment, the majority of the cities are in urban areas, not urban clusters or rural areas; they are in metropolitan areas, not micropolitan

Table 3.6

Technology Employers and Generators Employment by Location Characteristics

		Technology employers			
	Mean/Mode	Quartile 1	Quartile 2	Quartile 3	Quartile 4
Urban area/ cluster	UA	UA	UA	UA	UA
Principal city	NPC	NPC	NPC	NPC	NPC
Metropolitan/ micropolitan	Metro	Metro	Metro	Metro	Metro
Region	Midwest	Midwest	Midwest	South	West
		Technology generators			
	Mean/Mode	Quartile 1	Quartile 2	Quartile 3	Quartile 4
Urban area/ cluster	UA	UC	UA	UA	UA
Principal city	NPC	NPC	NPC	NPC	NPC
Metropolitan/ micropolitan	Metro	Metro	Metro	Metro	Metro
Region	Midwest	Midwest	South	Midwest	West

Sources: UA = urban area and UC = urban cluster (U.S. Census Bureau 2000c); NPC = not a principal city of the metropolitan or micropolitan statistical area (U.S. Census Bureau 2004); regions (U.S. Census Bureau 2002b).
Note: Significance levels = *** at 0.01, ** at 0.05, and * at 0.10.

areas; and they are not the principal cities of either metropolitan or micropolitan areas. For the most part, the mode for quartiles corresponds with the modal category for the whole sample. One location characteristic differs, but only for the technology generator sector—those cities with the least employment in the sector are in an urban cluster. Region, on the other hand, exhibits greater variation by quartile of employment, but only in the middle two quartiles. For technology employer employment, more cities in the second and third quartiles are located in the Midwest and South, respectively. The modal regions for the same quartiles are reversed for technology generators. This is interesting because the technology employer quartiles represent greater employment than the quartiles for technology generators; quartile two for technology employers (2.35 to 4.05 percent) covers a similar range as quartile three for technology generators (2.18 to 3.88 percent). Consequently, for cities in the Midwest, the employment range for both sectors is similar, even with the quartile difference, but for cities in the South, there is much less employment in technology generators (quartile two, 0.8 to 2.17 percent) than in technology employers (quartile three, 4.06 to 6.00 percent). The South seems to be a region that is more likely to attract technology employer industries. Nonetheless, the region capturing the greatest number of cities with the highest levels of technology employment in either sector is the West.

Technology Sectors and Infrastructure

The foregoing analysis provides some context in terms of the types of cities that are performing well in the technology economy. With regard to city economic characteristics, cities with greater proportions of technology sectors employment had, on average, stronger economic indicators, suggesting that the role of the technology economy in local economic development is important. This is particularly true for the demographics of the leading cities when considered relative to other research and from what we know about cities. The youthfulness and skilled population of some cities relative to others may indeed be factors that favor growth. Regional economists refer to the spatial succession or regional rotation of growth areas, where growth in one region increases costs of doing business for labor, land, and other inputs. The increased costs force mature industries to consider relatively cheaper locations. This is possible because as firms age, they often thwart the development of new ideas because their infrastructure ages and they become less able and willing to respond to new ideas. Production in mature industries becomes routine and not as dependent on innovation. Consequently, mature production industries filter down, or spatially rotate from skilled to unskilled regions. The regional rotation of mature industries suggests that new regions, or those suitable, will be where innovation is abundant (Malecki 1991, 1997). Cities with factors that lead to these advantages will most likely be at the beginning of the regional rotation. Yet the combination of innovation and human capital, as represented in the technology sectors, is only one building block of the technology economy. Understanding the other building block, technology infrastructure, in relation to how the cities are performing in technology sectors employment provides a more complete picture.

Although during the 2004 election cycle President George W. Bush made a call for greater broadband deployment that would be both universal and affordable by 2007, the Bush administration has not provided a vision or shown any type of effort to deliver on this call (Bleha 2005). In fact, from 2001 to 2003 the United States fell from fourth to thirteenth place in global broadband Internet penetration, according to the International Telecommunication Union (ITU) annual reports (International Telecommunication Union 2003; Bleha 2005). To make matters worse, the ITU's 2005 annual report shows another decline to sixteenth place, with the United States now lagging behind South Korea, Hong Kong, Canada, and Japan, to name a few (International Telecommunication Union 2005b). The Federal Communications Commission's (FCC) report on broadband deployment in 2004 states that there are 38 million subscribers to high-speed Internet in the United States; however, the speed of so-called high-speed lines is paltry in comparison to other options and offerings in other countries (Federal Communications Commission 2005). The FCC defines high speed as 200 kilobits per second, which is about five times slower than a standard DSL line and ten times slower than a cable modem. In fact, the speed of these lines is drastically slower than options found in countries like South Korea and Japan, where it also costs less than in the United States. For example, Thomas Bleha found that nearly all Japanese have an average connection speed that is sixteen times faster than in the United States for a relatively inexpensive price of $22 a month (Bleha 2005).

South Korea's national government has been very proactive in broadband. The South Korean government invested $400 million in a national high-speed fiber-optic backbone, mainly for national and local government, education, and research usage, but it was also meant to spur private broadband development. The country's 1997 Cyber Building Certificate program is a perfect example. The program enables local governments to issue certificates to real estate developers and building owners based on the speed of broadband service available in each housing unit. A three-tier system rates each household unit, with a tier 1 certificate ensuring broadband capacity above 50 Mbps (megabits per second), tier 2 ensuring 10 to 50 Mbps, and tier 3 providing broadband access under 10 Mbps. South Korea's government has incentivized broadband deployment throughout old and new housing developments, and developers use the certificates in advertisements to provide market differentiation (Lee, O'Keefe, and Yun 2003). These actions have led to intense telecommunications infrastructure competition, providing higher-quality services at lower prices, something the United States is lacking. The vast U.S. geography to some degree inhibits the quick deployment of infrastructure at a return on investment that is acceptable to most private telecommunications providers, yet even in large cities like New York, there are many areas where broadband services are not available (Center for an Urban Future 2004). The high-speed access problem is pervasive, and residential and small business customers (99.7 percent of all establishments in the United States) are suffering under these conditions (U.S. Small Business Administration 2004). "The economic impact of increased broadband availability may operate directly by attracting firms that rely on sophisticated telecommunications, or more indirectly by first attracting or promoting the development of residents who are technologically sophisticated, which in turn leads to firms locating in order to take advantage of the labor pool" (Clark et al. 2002). The recognition by local governments of these trends seems entrepreneurial, yet essential for a continued technology economy position, whether inside the United States or on a global stage.

The technology infrastructure comparison found in Table 3.7 touches upon a variety of technology infrastructure issues, from physical telecommunications measures to survey measures of local strategies and infrastructure assessment; each is an attempt to measure the capability of local technology infrastructure. The first measure of technology infrastructure, metropolitan bandwidth, does not account for the locality, but for the metropolitan area in which the city is located. The data report the telecommunications capacity or bandwidth that is available to a region from multiple telecommunications provider networks in megabits per second relative to the population of the metropolitan or micropolitan area.[16] Comparing metropolitan bandwidth for technology employers and generators reveals that higher levels of bandwidth, per population, might sometimes be available in lower-employment areas. Conversely, with local infrastructure, the relationships often change. The FCC requires all facilities-based telecommunications providers with at least 250 high-speed lines in a state to report the number of lines serviced on Form 477 as part of their data collection effort on local telephone competition and broadband deployment (Federal Communications Commission 2002). High-speed lines are connections that deliver services at speeds that exceed 200 kilobits per second in at least one direction. The broadband data are released by ZIP code yearly, and with similar manipulation as used for the employment data, the data are aggregated to the city level.[17] Cities with the greatest average number of high-speed lines per population have more employment in technology employer

Table 3.7

Technology Employers and Generators Employment by Technology Infrastructure

		Technology employers			
	Mean/Mode	Quartile 1	Quartile 2	Quartile 3	Quartile 4
Metropolitan bandwidth per pop.	0.107	0.061	0.159	0.135	0.085
High-speed lines per 1,000 pop.	0.175	0.160	0.184	0.162	0.206
High-speed lines per square mile	1.122**	0.506	1.286	1.225	1.649
Wireless towers per 1,000 pop.	0.095	0.087	0.098	0.118	0.081
Wireless towers per square mile	0.229*	0.135	0.233	0.241	0.316
Fiber available	Yes	Yes	Yes	Yes	Yes
Telecom improvements	Yes	Yes	Yes	Yes	Yes
Telecom inventory	No	No	No	No	No
Telecom ED plan	No	No	No	No	No
Telecom strategy usage	Yes	Yes	Yes	Yes	Yes

		Technology generators			
	Mean/Mode	Quartile 1	Quartile 2	Quartile 3	Quartile 4
Metropolitan bandwidth per pop.	0.107	0.160	0.057	0.131	0.084
High-speed lines per 1,000 pop.	0.175	0.191	0.153	0.170	0.185
High-speed lines per square mile	1.122**	0.459	1.261	0.981	1.561
Wireless towers per 1,000 pop.	0.095	0.106	0.078	0.112	0.089
Wireless towers per square mile	0.229*	0.157	0.160	0.267	0.304
Fiber available	Yes	Yes	Yes	Yes	Yes
Telecom improvements	Yes	Yes	Yes	Yes	Yes
Telecom inventory	No	No	No	No	No
Telecom ED plan	No	No	No	No	No
Telecom strategy usage	Yes	Yes	Yes	Yes	Yes

Sources: Bandwidth (Gorman 2004); high-speed lines (Federal Communications Commission 2002); wireless towers (SpectraSite 2004); remaining variables from survey (Hacker 2002).

Note: Significance levels = *** at 0.01, ** at 0.05, and * at 0.10.

industries; however, the relationship is reversed for technology generators—the most high-speed lines are in cities with the smallest proportion of employment in the sector. High-speed lines per square mile exhibit a very different relationship. This measure is statistically different for all four quartiles of both technology sectors and is also highest for cities with the largest employment in technology employers and generators, 1.649 and 1.561, respectively. The result suggests that the physical size of the locale matters, and the availability of high-speed providers is limited.

The final piece of physical infrastructure data compared is wireless towers. The wireless towers data are measured in terms of both population and land density, and include all wireless towers—cell, rooftop, in-building, and broadcast (SpectraSite 2004).[18] For wireless infrastructure, both density measures are consistent with the analysis of high-speed lines. For the wireless towers relative to population, there is not a clear relationship between the number of towers per person and employment in technology employers and generators. However, for wireless towers per square mile, there is, indicating once again that physical space is important. It should be noted that while these differences are significant, the actual number of towers per mile or for the population is very small.

The lack of density for both DSL and wireless towers is a telecommunications issue that the federal government has chosen to leave in the private market's hands, yet the pace of the private providers seems sluggish. Cities are noticing. Many cities are coming forward with a variety of publicly funded and sometimes publicly operated networks, both wireless and wire line. In 2005, five large cities signaled that it is the public sector's role to provide their citizens with essential services, of which broadband is one. Boston mayor Thomas Menino recently drove around the city to determine the quality of its wireless phone coverage ("All Things Considered" 2005; Estes 2005). Declaring it dismal, Mayor Menino believes that Boston should try to find a way to improve this infrastructure. Menino also went on record stating that wireless Internet should be available within four years anywhere in Boston, and he is hoping that public and private partnerships will help him reach this goal (St. Martin 2005). The other four cities, Denver, Minneapolis, Philadelphia, and Portland (Oregon), have actually released requests for proposals for the creation of wireless networks that would provide broadband for their cities. Each city is looking at a number of options, from public to public-private partnerships. At this point in time, Philadelphia and Portland have awarded the contracts for their citywide wireless networks, and Minneapolis has chosen two finalists. These companies will pilot their networks so that the city can make a final selection.

As one example, Unwire Portland, the city's wireless Internet project, is interested in a private wholesale model, where a private company would build the network throughout the city, especially to publicly owned buildings. However, the private company would continue to operate the network in a wholesale manner such that all Internet service providers would be able to lease network capacity. The project would serve to increase the wireless telecommunications options in Portland and assist with both economic development and social objectives. To make the project attractive, the city of Portland would streamline the permitting process and subsidize access to traffic signals and rooftops, making it easier for the private company to contract for space to install equipment. The city would also look to move a number of its current institutional network contracts to this wireless network if the private company can support the applications at a level of security and redundancy the city would require. There is also the promise of new applications, like the operation of city parking meters. People could use a credit card to pay for all parking over an application that uses the wireless network. Portland would not place any restrictions on the type of wireless network technologies, but would instead voice its preference for the types of applications and functions it would need to support. The city believes that the private company has it in its best interest to build a network that would be able to meet these demands and provide access to additional providers to increase the success of and profits from the project (Ahmed 2005).

As another example, UTOPIA, the Utah Telecommunications Open Infrastructure Agency, is an interlocal agreement of fourteen cities in central Utah seeking to provide better telecommunications options. The consortium of cities will own the UTOPIA Community MetroNet, an ultra-broadband fiber-optic network that will provide access to approximately 140,000 homes and will be built in three phases. UTOPIA secured $85 million in municipal bonds to finance and begin Phase I of the network in August 2004.[19] UTOPIA selected Tetra Tech to perform the installation, with the first phase to be finished in the summer of 2007 and the second phase scheduled to begin in the first quarter of 2006. AT&T and MSTAR.NET are the first two telecommunications providers that will offer a range of voice, video, and data services to customers. UTOPIA is unique because it is a consortium of cities that are looking for enhanced telecommunications services to improve both economic development opportunities and quality of life, claiming that the cities will be attractive places in which to live and to locate businesses because of the enormous speed and capability of the fiber-optic network. UTOPIA has also ensured that the construction of the network will mean more jobs to local residents. Tetra Tech will employ mostly local workers to do the final engineering and the physical deployment of the fiber ring, and Communications Technology Services, Inc., will hire local workers to wire the network from the utility easement in the street to the home or business. UTOPIA's selection of MSTAR.NET is also strategic for the area since it is one of the largest Internet service providers in Utah (Utah Telecommunications Open Infrastructure Agency 2005). UTOPIA and Unwire Portland are just two examples of a multitude of cities in the United States seeking to improve their telecommunications services and tying these improvements to other economic and social goals.

The Economic Development and Technology Economy Survey of economic development officials in cities attempted to gain systematic and comparative data on local actions in telecommunications to determine how these are related to economic development. Chapter 4 discusses the results of the survey more fully, but several of the survey items are relevant vis-à-vis the technology sectors comparison (Table 3.7). In order to understand what cities have in terms of telecommunications infrastructure, local economic development officials reported on the availability of multiple wire-line and wireless options. However, the problem with such reporting of availability, given the locations of most of the cities, is that there was very little variation in these measures. For example, a large majority of cities have fiber-optic networks available (83 percent). As shown in Table 3.7, this measure accounts for little variation across both technology employer and technology generator employment. Also consistent across the sectors' employment quartiles is that cities report they have had recent improvements to their infrastructure—upgrades and additional miles of fiber or installation of wireless towers. Interestingly, local officials know it is available, but few seem to know the location of the infrastructure. Across the quartiles for technology employer or technology generator employment, the majority of cities reported having no inventory or knowledge of where and what bandwidth capacity is available from these telecommunications options. The lack of knowledge about the details of the telecommunications infrastructure seems to affect the long-term planning process of many cities. Although across the employment quartiles for both sectors, cities admit that they will use telecommunications in some type of strategy—from creating special telecommunications-ready office spaces to possibly deploying a fiber-optic network for a specific area or business—they also report that they do not address telecommunications in their economic development plans. A disconnect exists between integrating telecommunications knowledge and deployment strategies into an overall economic development process for the majority of cities. The findings on policy and infrastructure are the same across the technology sectors.

The analysis of city characteristics points to a variety of relationships among a city's employment in the technology sectors, technology infrastructure, and socioeconomic characteristics. However, further characterization of these relationships is essential if localities are to understand how these factors might help their cities to secure a place in the technology economy. To address these relationships, I conducted a series of regression analyses, presented below.

Factors Driving Technology Economy Success of Cities

The foremost responsibility of local economic development officials and practitioners is to design policies and strategies that create an environment in which economic growth and development can occur. Although improving the quality of life is a developmental spillover, most measure their success with job creation, and not just any type of job, but those that provide higher pay and benefits to employees. The current trend in economic growth and development policies is to seek and promote growth of targeted industries or clusters (Bradshaw and Blakely 1999; Porter 1998). Technology economy industries are a likely target because these industries offer higher wages to their employees, which in turn generate higher tax revenues for cities. In addition, technology industries are known to agglomerate in certain regions. Many cities seek these industries to gain technology reputations, like the Silicon Valley cities in northern California, Boston with its surrounding Route 128, and Austin, Texas, with its Silicon Hills. However, local economic development officials that desire such growth must create conditions that will allow new firms to take root and flourish (Blakely 1994). The analysis of city characteristics by employment indicates that cities with greater employment in the technology sectors have certain characteristics. In addition, the de-fining characteristics of the technology sectors make it likely that these industries require more than a basic core infrastructure. The human capital and innovation foundations of these industries will find cities that pro-vide an environment that fosters a sound research base, where inven-tion, adoption, development, innovation, and dissemination of products and services can occur. The role that the technology economy's infra-structure plays relative to other city characteristics may indeed be a fac-tor that local economic development officials need to better understand.

Building from the analysis of city characteristics, I examine the ef-fects of the local characteristics on employment in the technology sec-tors. I develop three regression models to predict employment in each of the technology sectors based on the city characteristics that produced statistically significant differences among the quartiles of employment in cities (Tables 3.4 through 3.7). Consequently, the sets of city charac-teristics for each model are slightly different. The black population in cities differed significantly by quartiles of technology employer em-ployment, such that cities with greater technology employer employ-ment had significantly smaller black populations. However, for technology generator employment, the differences among quartiles were not significant. In addition, a city's age demographic also varied for the two sectors; cities with high employment in the technology employer sector have significantly smaller aging populations (over age 64), while the younger population (ages 25 to 34) varies significantly in cities with respect to technology generator employment. The regression models include only the socioeconomic characteristics that have a significant differential among employment quartiles.[20]

One additional specific about the regression models is important to note. Several economic characteristics were significant for both sectors; however, the unemployment rate, per capita income, median household income, poverty, and housing affordability measures are not included separately in the regression models because some of these variables are measuring the same effects, namely the relative wealth of a jurisdiction. This leads to severe multicollinearity in the model. I conducted a series of statistical tests and determined that median household income pro-vides the best measure, and it is the only measure that is significantly correlated with each of the other variables. With this modification, I estimate three models for both technology sectors, with a city's percent employment in the technology sector as the dependent variable. The first model includes only the significant economic, demographic, and location characteristics for each sector as independent variables. The second model includes this set of independent variables with the two physical telecommunications infrastructure measures that were significant —high-speed lines and wireless towers per square mile. Finally, the third model examines one other permutation. Although no significant variation existed among technology sector employment for the infrastructure measures from the survey, these measures are important because of their link to local policy options that may have an effect in the technology economy. The third model includes these policy infrastructure measures with the other infrastructure and city characteristics from models one and two. I estimate the final regression models with OLS,[21] using a weighted least-squares correction for the heteroscedastic effect of patents on the standard errors and resulting t-stats for the coefficients of the independent variables.[22] Condition indices and variance decomposition proportions indicate that a minimal but acceptable level of multicollinearity exists.[23] The results of the six estimations are in Table 3.8.

The results for Model 1 exhibit the basic relationship for each city characteristic while controlling for the other factors. This baseline model indicates that technology employment in both technology sectors is highly correlated with both the number of patents and percentage of college graduates in the city. For every 1 percent increase in patents granted relative to city population, employment in technology employers increases 0.463 percent and employment in technology generators increases 0.428 percent. For every 1 percent increase in the number of college graduates in a city, technology employer employment increases 0.099 percent and technology generator employment increases 0.070 percent. Patents and college attainment capture the city's level of innovation and human capital, which are both integral in the definition of the two sectors. However, it is still interesting to see the strong positive correlation with employment in both sectors, while controlling for other factors, because the inventions for these patents in the city over the previous decade could have been invented outside of these technology industries. The strong positive correlation of the percentage of college graduates living in the city with technology employment has a similar interpretation. The majority of these college graduates may not be employed as scientists or engineers, or they may not be working in these industries because local labor markets are often regional in nature. Nonetheless, the education level or human capital capacity of a city is an important indi-

Table 3.8

Technology Employers and Generators Employment Regressed on Influencing Factors

	Technology employers			Technology generators		
	Model 1	Model 2	Model 3	Model 1	Model 2	Model 3
Patents per 1,000 population	0.463***	0.534***	0.534***	0.428***	0.473***	0.454***
	(0.071)	(0.074)	(0.078)	(0.061)	(0.058)	(0.059)
Median household income	2.771e-5	1.463e-5	1.245e-5	7.796e-5	1.247e-5	2.0668e-5
	(1.829e-5)	(2.015e-5)	(2.149e-5)	(1.456e-5)	(1.438e-5)	(1.507e-5)
% College graduates	0.099***	0.090***	0.093***	0.070***	0.057**	0.058**
	(0.031)	(0.031)	(0.033)	(0.026)	(0.025)	(0.025)
% Black	.008	0.003	0.001			
	(0.010)	(0.012)	(0.012)			
% Age 25–34				0.218***	0.285***	0.353***
				(0.066)	(0.083)	(0.088)
% Over age 64	-0.019	-0.070	-0.110**			
	(0.033)	(0.046)	(0.147)			
Region	0.353**	0.399**	0.465**	0.226*	0.320**	0.386**
	(0.159)	(0.184)	(0.212)	(0.130)	(0.141)	(0.158)
High-speed lines per square mile		0.236*	0.262*		0.023	0.016
		(0.142)	(0.147)		(0.110)	(0.112)

Wireless towers per square mile		0.756		0.590	0.334	0.203
		(0.572)		(0.600)	(0.443)	(0.452)
Telecom inventory				0.056		0.029
				(0.074)		(0.054)
Telecom ED plan				-0.036		0.024
				(0.316)		(0.240)
Telecom strategy usage				0.150		0.190**
				(0.124)		(0.092)
Telecom improvements				-0.212**		-0.139**
				(0.087)		(0.065)
Constant	-0.088	0.577	-2.445***	1.098	-3.634***	-4.845***
	(0.985)	(1.156)	(0.900)	(1.281)	(1.076)	(1.167)
Adjusted R squared	0.374	0.505	0.362	0.533	0.536	0.580
F-statistic	25.957	22.202	29.429	14.895	28.422	19.316
Number of cities	252	167	252	147	167	147

Note: Significance levels *** at 0.01, ** at 0.05, and * at 0.10. Standard Errors of the unstandardized coefficients are in parentheses. The number of cities differ in the three models due to lack of data for all or some of the physical and policy-related telecommunications infrastructure measures in a city. See Tables 3.4 through 3.7 for sources.

cator of employment in the technology economy sectors. As explained in Chapter 2, the importance of understanding this relationship at the local level is consequential. It is at the city level that government has financial and policy powers, and officials are often appointed by elected representatives to create a city that is successful and livable. Local economic development practitioners can use the knowledge that technology employers are more likely to meet their workforce needs in cities that have higher-quality human capital. Structuring and influencing local educational institutions and helping design programs with partners that promote higher learning and skills attainment are important local strategies to continue to produce human capital and attract individuals who want such educational opportunities for their children. For example, the city of Riverside formed a public-private partnership with the county credit union and a local computer business to help low-income students qualify for technology jobs by helping them obtain high-quality computers and training. These actions are likely to also have a positive effect on the level of innovation in the community.[24] The regression results suggest that a locality's promotion and support of these factors is important to technology sector employment.

Turning to the other factors, the age of the population is significant only in the technology generators base model. Cities with a large percentage of the population between the ages of 25 and 34 years have greater employment in the technology generator sector. For every one percent increase in this population, technology generator employment increases 0.218 percent, holding all other factors constant. More often than not, the younger segment of a city is at the cusp of its economic productivity. Many of this age are graduated from college and beginning graduate programs, starting jobs, or possibly starting a business of their own—13.1 percent were self-employed in 2002 (U.S. Small Business Administration 2004). This population brings both energy and opportunity to most cities due in some part to what Florida refers to as the "new social construction of time," or how the use of our time during the course of our lives is very different than preceding generations. Currently, many front-load their careers, packing the "most intense and productive creative work into their younger years, when their potential for advancement and sheer physical energy are at a peak" (Florida 2002, 14). The creative and innovative culture of this younger population is beneficial to a city's environment, while at the same time these are citizens who often demand the least from cities in terms of services. The combination of these traits may make cities with youthful populations more attractive to technology generator businesses. At the other extreme, the older population, over sixty-four years of age, is a factor in the technology employer employment models because of its significance in the quartile analysis. The older population measure is significant only in Model 3 for technology employers, and unlike the younger population, the older population has a negative correlation with city employment in the technology employers sector, yet indicates a similar overall relationship. Employment in both technology sectors is greater in cities with more youthful populations, suggesting that such cities may be superior locations for technology industries.

Region of the United States is the final characteristic that has a significant effect on employment, for both sectors. Cities in specific regions have greater employment in the technology sectors. The significant factors in the baseline models for both technology employers and technology generators remain significant and carry the same positive correlations with employment in the other two models. Given these consistent results, the remaining discussion of the regressions concentrates on the telecommunications infrastructure variables.

The first introduction of telecommunications infrastructure depicts physical telecommunications measures in Model 2, and the adjusted R-squared statistics for both technology sectors' estimations indicate a substantial increase in the explanatory power of Model 2. Local telecommunications infrastructure is an important factor in explaining local sector employment. However, the model reveals that technology generators are very different from technology employers with respect to physical telecommunications infrastructure. Neither high-speed line nor wireless tower land density is correlated with employment in technology generator industries. Yet the direct effect of more high-speed lines per square mile is positive in the model for technology employers. Technology employer employment is greater in such cities. For every additional increment in high-speed line density, technology employer employment increases 0.236 percent, although the level of significance is approaching the cutoff. Nevertheless, high-speed line density remains positively correlated and significant to technology employer employment in the last and third model with the addition of the policy-related telecommunications infrastructure variables.

In Model 3, the introduction of the policy-related telecommunications infrastructure variables provides clarification to the considerable difference between technology sectors in regard to the relationship among employment and the types telecommunications infrastructures. Technology employer employment is correlated with a physical infrastructure measure (high-speed line density), but with only one of the policy-related infrastructure measures. The opposite holds true for technology generators, with employment in these industries correlated with two policy-related infrastructure measures, but none of the physical infrastructure measures. Physical telecommunications infrastructure is often in the hands of private telecommunications providers, and local governments are not able to directly affect the planning and deployment of upgrades or extra capacity. Conversely, local governments do have control of the policy-related measures. The one policy measure that is significant in both models of technology sectors employment is telecommunications improvements, which assesses whether a city has made improvements or not. The survey question asked policymakers to include any improvements after the Telecommunications Act of 1996, both nongovernmental and governmental telecommunications initiatives, so a portion of this measure represents private telecommunications deployments and a portion represents governmental deployments (Telecommunications Act of 1996, 1996). Consequently, this measure has both physical infrastructure and policy dimensions. The latter is a result of government taking action in this traditionally private sector space. What is most interesting about this measure is that regardless of whether the telecommunications improvements were a result of nongovernmental or governmental action, the improvements measure is negatively correlated with employment in both the technology employer and technology generator sectors. The telecommunications improvements measure is a dichotomous dummy variable, as are the other policy infrastructure measures. Consequently, the interpretation is slightly different because a dummy variable affects the intercept term—the mean of employment—not the slope coefficients. The total direct effect of the telecommunications improvements variable requires that the coefficient on the significant dummy variable be added to the coefficient of the constant, but only when the constant is significant. In Model 3 for technology employers, the constant is not significant, and thus not different from zero. The interpretation is that for cities with telecommunications improvements, the mean of the technology employer employment is 0.212 percent less than for cities without improvements. In the case of technology generators, the constant's coefficient is significant, so the telecommunications improvements coefficient (-0.139) is added to the constant (-4.845). In cities with telecommunications improvements, the mean technology generator employment is -4.984, which is 0.139 percent less than cities without improvements.

Only one of the other three policy-related telecommunications infrastructure measures significantly affects employment, and only for the technology generator sector. Unlike the telecommunications improvements measure, the fact that a city utilizes telecommunications in its economic development strategies is positively correlated with employment for technology generator industries, correcting for the influence of all other characteristics in Model 3. Local economic development officials responded to whether they used telecommunications infrastructure as a tool or asset in promoting economic development. This could include policies such as deploying fiber-optic networks, creation of technology zones and telecommunications incubators, designing smart buildings that are equipped with advanced telecommunications services, or providing regulatory flexibility or tax incentives to telecommunications providers. Cities that consider telecommunications infrastructure as an asset and design economic development strategies around it have 0.190 percent greater employment than cities without such strategies, such that cities with this policy mindset have a larger mean technology employment (-4.655) than cities without it.[25]

Overall, the telecommunications infrastructure measures have a more positive than negative effect on employment in the technology sectors, while providing a substantial increase in the explanatory power of the models. Local physical infrastructure is more likely to affect technology employers, while policy integrating infrastructure into economic development plans is more likely to affect technology generators, yet both sectors exhibit negative relationships with infrastructure improvements. One possible interpretation of the negative effect of telecommunications improvements is that these cities may have possessed inferior telecommunications infrastructure in their jurisdictions in comparison to other cities during the same time period. Even with the improvements, these cities may not be as well off from a telecommunications infrastructure perspective. Given the positive correlations among employment in the technology sectors and other telecommunications infrastructure measures, the industries in these sectors may prefer cities with better-than-average telecommunications infrastructure. If so, cities in need of improvements would not be as likely locations for such industries, although presumably those improvements could eventually make the cities more attractive.

The analyses presented in this chapter provide a snapshot of the characteristics of cities that are leading in the technology economy sectors. Cities in which technology employers have a larger employment presence are more innovative and well educated, with a smaller older population. In addition, these cities have greater high-speed line density, but fewer telecommunications improvements than cities lagging in technology employer employment. Physical telecommunications infrastructure has an impact. Cities leading in technology generator employment are also more innovative and well educated, and they have a large young adult population. Local officials in these cities think about and use their telecommunications infrastructure as part of economic development strategies, but these cities have had fewer telecommunications improvements than cities lagging in technology generator employment. The differences by sector indicate where cities can possibly focus—whether by developing human capital or innovative capacity. Additionally, local telecommunications infrastructure is an important factor in explaining local sector employment; therefore, there is some evidence of relationships between the two building blocks of the technology economy—the sectors and the infrastructure. How cities capitalize on this relationship is essential to their futures in the technology economy. Chapter 4 will present more on how city officials view the relationship between the technology economy and economic development, as well as current infrastructure capacities and improvement.

4

Economic Development and the Technology Economy in Cities

In this economic environment, typified by increasingly mobile global capital, it is argued that enhancing place-based characteristics of infrastructure, education, and lifestyle make up the few remaining goals that government may realistically undertake. However, national or state governments may not be the best positioned to advance these objectives. . . . Cities . . . may have a more appropriate role in providing communications, transportation and other physical infrastructures, educational, research and technology institutions, and a lifestyle to attract a trained and capable workforce in order to draw and retain mobile global capital. Cities and local governments have noted these developments in their planning, and have promoted the use of telecommunications infrastructure as a local advantage.

—Stephen D. McDowell

Telecommunications infrastructure investment . . . may be the most significant investment decision that public sector leaders can influence.

—Thomas W. Bonnett

Cities are key actors in the deployment of technology economy infrastructure. Cities play a role in the location decisions of technology economy businesses, industries, and economic sectors. Following the lead of the Silicon Valley, examples abound of cities and regions adopting economic development strategies focused on becoming the next technology economy center—whether it is the noted success of the Silicon Gulch/Hills area surrounding Austin, Texas, and Route 128 in the Boston area, or lesser-known efforts like the Silicon Prairie in the Stillwater, Oklahoma area, Silicon Hollow in Oak Ridge, Tennessee, and the Silicon Glacier in the Kalispell, Montana area. In all of these cases, technology economy growth is a target, and cities across the United States are seeking to establish a niche in this perceived growth arena. Regardless of whether cities are at the top or the bottom of the rankings of technology economy employers and generators, most cities recognize a need to invest in technology economy infrastructure as an economic development strategy.

What types of activities do cities undertake, both to develop technology economy infrastructure and to attract technology economy sectors? To answer this question, a direct mail survey of city economic development officials was conducted in 2002. The Economic Development and Technology Economy Survey was sent to the lead economic development official in every city over 50,000 in population and to a random sample of lead economic development officials in cities under 50,000 in population. A special emphasis on the larger cities was necessary for two reasons: first, because the scale of resources devoted to economic development activities across the municipal sector is likely to be dominated by the largest cities, and second, because the relatively small number of cities over 50,000[1] requires that the sample include all of these cities in order to ensure an adequate response rate.[2] I compared the responding 252 cities against the national population of cities and weighted the responses accordingly in order to ensure that the sample is representative, to the extent possible, of cities nationwide.[3]

The survey was looking for answers to the following questions:

- What is the role of technology economy infrastructure and industry development in the local economies of cities?
- To what extent do cities' economic development strategies include technology economy infrastructure development and business attraction targets?
- What is the current state and capacity of technology economy infrastructure in cities?
- What types of infrastructure improvements have been made or are planned?

Economic Development in Cities

Economic development in cities is a big business. Cities devote significant amounts of resources—dollars and staff—to economic development activities. The average economic development budget for the cities responding to the Economic Development and Technology Economy Survey was $1.7 million, ranging from cities that reported no economic

Table 4.1

Full-Time City Economic Development Staff (*N* = 251)

	All cities (%)
More than 5 employees	21
3–5 employees	20
Less than 3 employees	59

Table 4.2

Impact of Economic Development on Jobs (*N* = 247)

	All cities (%)
Increased job growth	79
No impact	5
Don't know	16

development budget to cities with $550 million devoted to economic development activities. Many cities also have significant staff investments in economic development and redevelopment. Two in five economic development officials (41 percent) reported that their cities devote more than three full-time employees solely to these purposes (see Table 4.1).

Cities' investment in economic development tends to have two primary targets—*attraction* of business and industry, and *retention* of existing business and industry. Economic development officials reported that 70 percent of economic development staff time is devoted to business attraction (37 percent) and retention (33 percent) in their cities. Attracting and retaining business has a number of payoffs for cities—the provision of jobs for residents and nonresidents, attraction of new residents who come to fill job openings, and enhancement of city tax bases as new business and individual taxpayers contribute to city budgets.

Jobs, in the end, often represent the biggest payoff. When asked if they think their cities' economic development efforts resulted in increased job growth, 79 percent of economic development officials said yes, 16 percent said that they did not know, and only 5 percent said no (see Table 4.2). On average, the 247 economic development officials that responded to the question said that over 900 jobs had been created as a result of city economic development efforts, ranging from as few as ten jobs to more than 73,000 jobs in individual cities.

Table 4.3

Types of Jobs Created

	All cities (%)	N
Full- vs. Part-time		
Full-time	99	188
Part-time	65	185
Higher- vs. lower-wage		
Higher-wage	82	188
Lower-wage	83	185
Higher- vs. lower-skill		
Higher-skill	78	188
Lower-skill	83	185

The types of jobs created also matters. Given a choice, most city officials would probably express a preference for full-time, higher-wage, higher-skilled jobs, and economic development officials reported that city economic development efforts are successful on all three fronts—99 percent reported the creation of full-time jobs, 82 percent higher-wage jobs, and 78 percent higher-skilled jobs. Differences in city labor markets might also require a diversity of jobs, and economic development officials reported the creation of part-time (65 percent), lower-wage (83 percent), or lower-skilled (83 percent) jobs as well (see Table 4.3).

Where do technology economy infrastructure and technology economy business attraction and retention fit into these city economic development efforts? The unprecedented economic growth generated by technology economy sectors over the past two decades undoubtedly resulted in changes in city economic development strategies targeting this new source of growth—evidenced by city officials packaging their cities as the Silicon Snowbank (Minneapolis–St. Paul, Minnesota) or Silicon Sandbar (Cape Cod, Massachusetts). Cities responding to the survey expressed anticipation of growth in technology economy industries. When asked which sector best described their economic base over the previous five years in comparison to their predictions for the next five years, the percentage of economic development officials that pointed to technology economy sectors increased from 1.5 percent to 7.8 percent. To shed light on cities' technology economy–targeting activities, I turn next to an analysis of economic development officials' views about the role of the technology economy in their local economies. I then examine current city capacities in terms of technology economy infrastructure and improvements.

Table 4.4

Technology Economy Fit in Local Economies

Responses to the question "Where does the technology economy fit into your local economy?" (%)

	Best fit	2nd Best fit	N
Critical infrastructure that facilitates other sectors	68	22	172
As an economic sector	20	50	214
As an undeveloped factor	36	18	175

The Technology Economy's Role in Local Economies

Cities' economic development efforts are obviously not limited to targeting technology economy growth. Most cities are likely to use strategies that yield a diversified economic base for the city, with different types of industries providing different types of jobs. The technology economy is one piece of the economic equation and economic development officials' views about its role in their local economies are likely to vary based on local circumstances. For some, given technology economy growth over the last decade in particular, there might be greater emphasis on growing this particular area.

When asked where the technology economy fits into their local economy, economic development officials said that they see the technology economy as being about critical infrastructure first and as being an economic sector second (see Table 4.4). Economic development officials are most likely to see "critical infrastructure that facilitates other sectors" (68 percent) as the description that best fits their view, as opposed to seeing the technology economy "as an economic sector" (20 percent) or "as an undeveloped factor" (36 percent). The description characterized by development officials as the second best fit is "as an economic sector" (50 percent), compared to "critical infrastructure . . ." (22 percent), and "an undeveloped factor" (18 percent).

In terms of the technology economy's contribution to their locality's future economic viability, most (57 percent) economic development officials said that it is an "essential component." Four in ten (39 percent) indicated that the technology economy is a component in their local economy, but not necessarily essential to economic viability. Only 2 percent said that the technology economy is not relevant to their city's economic health.

Cities pursue technology economy advances for reasons beyond economic development, such as improving day-to-day operations in the city through efficiency and productivity gains. For example, a host of online technological improvements, often broadly referred to as e-government services, have a growing presence in cities. Many cities now make a multitude of forms available on their websites (for example, applications for special permits or licenses), post notices of important information (public meetings, events), or have systems to log and track public complaints. When asked how important technology economy-related services are to the daily operations of their cities, economic development officials overwhelmingly said that these services are important. Nine in ten officials (89 percent) said that such services are either very important (47 percent) or relatively important (42 percent).

While city officials indicate that the technology economy is seen as critical infrastructure for economic development, as an important economic sector, and as important to the daily operations of their cities, few reported that their cities have an economic development plan in place that addresses technology economy infrastructure. Three in four economic development officials (77 percent) said that their city has no such plan, compared to 21 percent that reported having a technology economy development plan. However, nearly half (47 percent) of the officials reporting that their city lacks such a plan said that they intend to develop a plan in the next two years (see Table 4.5). Comments provided by the responding officials, in an effort to explain the lack of plans, pointed to concerns about crafting plans to adequately meet business needs, when in many cases the expected businesses were not yet located in the jurisdiction and so their needs may not have been transparent; a lack of individual expertise on technology issues within the economic development staff or offices; and a desire to wait for the rapid development of new technologies to slow down or stabilize, to some degree, so that the available options for cities would be easier to identify and the advantages and disadvantages more apparent. In addition, respondents raised questions about whether their cities need to fulfill this role, or whether providers in the private sector would move first to provide technology economy infrastructure. The development of the technology economy overall is a relatively recent phenomenon, coming to the fore primarily in the past decade, so it is not surprising that cities' involvement in the technology economy arena is still developing. Forty-eight of the surveyed economic development officials who reported that their cities have

Table 4.5

Existence of Technology Economy Plans in Cities

	All cities (%)	N
Existing plan		247
Yes	21	52
No	77	190
Don't know	2	5
Will develop in next 2 years		170
Yes	47	80
No	12	20
Don't know	41	70

a technology economy plan were able to specify when the plan was initially developed. The most common response was 2001 (28 percent), followed by 1998 (17 percent), and 2000 (15 percent). Overall, when it comes to planning efforts at the city level, increased awareness of the technology economy's impact on cities is apparent, but adoption of strategies to address how cities can best harness the technology economy is lacking.

For those cities taking action, what do their economic development plans include in terms of technology economy strategies? The two most common strategies cited by economic development officials are using the Internet and city websites to advertise and promote the location (82 percent) and deploying fiber-optic cable (62 percent). Three in ten economic development officials also identified the creation of "smart buildings" (32 percent)—buildings equipped with advanced telecommunications services and technologies—or telecommunications or technology incubators (29 percent)—for example, city-facilitated services and office space to help small technology and telecommunications businesses and startups with marketing, research and development, and office needs. One in five cities' plans also seek to create technology zones (19 percent), provide tax incentives (18 percent), or ease regulatory requirements on telecommunications providers (18 percent) (see Table 4.6).

A number of factors could potentially prevent the inclusion of technology economy infrastructure in cities' economic development strategies. One set of factors has to do with the fact that cities are not the only set of actors in this arena. The private sector often serves as the provider of first resort, letting the market drive where the infrastructure is deployed. Indeed, many cities' involvement in the provision of technology economy infrastructure is driven by the lack of provision by the private

Table 4.6

Elements of City Technology Economy Development Plans (N = 219)

	All cities (%)
Internet/website used to advertise and promote locale	82
Deployment of fiber-optic cable/network	62
Smart buildings	32
Telecommunications/technology incubators	29
Technology zones	19
Tax incentives for telecommunications providers	18
Regulatory flexibility for telecommunications providers	18

sector or is a means of filling gaps. The state and federal governments are not necessarily passive participants either. State governments and the federal government have actively regulated and preempted, or attempted to regulate and preempt, local authority to deploy technology economy infrastructure.[4] Regardless of the role of the private sector and other levels of government, a number of factors internal to the city might also prevent cities from having a role in technology economy infrastructure. Lack of funding is sure to be one concern, as cities must balance competing needs and demands for services. In some cases, there might not be sufficient support within the government to invest in technology economy infrastructure, or there might be bureaucratic practices that impede activity in this arena (such as planning and permit processes).

When asked about hurdles preventing their cities' use of technology economy infrastructure as part of economic development strategies, economic development officials most often cited lack of funding (69 percent) as a hurdle, followed by private sector ownership of the infrastructure (35 percent), federal and/or state regulatory control (20 percent), and lack of local government support (15 percent). Only 5 percent of economic development officials indicated that planning bodies' control of permitting was a hurdle (see Table 4.7).

Technology Economy Infrastructure in Cities

The technology economy is clearly seen as critical local infrastructure and as a target for economic development activities, as indicated by the responses from economic development officials. Yet, despite this perceived importance, few cities seem to have developed and implemented targeted strategies, in the form of economic development plans, for de-

Table 4.7

Hurdles to City Involvement in the Technology Economy (*N* = 200)

	All cities (%)
Lack of funding	69
Private sector ownership	35
Federal/State regulatory control	20
Lack of local government support	15
Planning and permitting controls	5

Table 4.8

Availability of Technology Economy Infrastructure in Cities (*N* = 252)
Percentage responding "yes" to the question of whether infrastructure is available

	All cities (%)
Fiber-optic cable	84
Coaxial/Hybrid fiber coax	71
Wireless towers	72
Microwave transmitters	42
Satellite facilities	48

ploying information technology and telecommunications infrastructure and targeting technology economy industry. This disconnect between perceptions and planning raises a key question: What is the current state and capacity of technology economy infrastructure in cities?

City economic development officials were asked about whether five standard types of technology economy infrastructure were available in their cities—fiber-optic cable, coaxial/hybrid fiber coax, wireless towers, fixed wireless/microwave transmitters, and satellite facilities (all five are described in detail in Chapter 2). The two wire-line options—fiber-optic cable (84 percent) and coaxial/hybrid fiber coax (71 percent)—and wireless towers (72 percent) were most often cited as being available in cities. The other wireless options, microwave transmitters (42 percent) and satellite facilities (48 percent), were cited as being comparatively less common (see Table 4.8).

In most cases, the availability of infrastructure is dependent upon provision by a number of different actors. Telephone companies, telecommunications providers (e.g., cable and satellite companies), and utilities are often the first to provide telecommunications infrastructure in cities. Local governments may also provide infrastructure, often driven

Table 4.9

Ownership of Technology Economy Infrastructure in Cities

| | | Ownership (%) | | |
	N	Local government	Telephone company	Telecom provider	Utility
Fiber-optic cable	209	16	77	50	15
Coaxial/hybrid fiber coax	180	5	23	67	16
Wireless towers	183	9	36	67	7
Microwave transmitters	105	17	30	51	12
Satellite facilities	121	3	10	60	7

Note: Percentages will not add to 100 because multiple types of owners may simultaneously own various infrastructures.

by the lack of infrastructure or gaps in service, as suggested earlier. City economic development officials were most likely to cite telecommunications companies as owning various types of infrastructure, including coaxial/hybrid fiber coax (67 percent), wireless towers (67 percent), satellite facilities (60 percent), and microwave transmitters (51 percent). The lone exception was fiber-optic cable, which economic development officials indicated was more likely to be owned by telephone companies (77 percent) than other providers. Local governments were cited as being smaller players in terms of ownership of technology economy infrastructure. Local government ownership was most often cited in the areas of microwave transmitters (17 percent) and fiber-optic cable (16 percent) (see Table 4.9).

For any provider of technology economy infrastructure, public or private, access to or control of rights-of-way is necessary in order to install and monitor the infrastructure. Technically, right-of-way is the legal right to pass over land owned by another entity. Local governments often own the rights-of-way needed to deploy infrastructure. These rights-of-way are most often thought of as the streets and roads under which fiber-optic cable are laid, but also might include the buildings and rooftops on which wireless towers are placed, or utility poles and other radio towers often used for various wireless infrastructures. Many of these rights-of-way are publicly owned and maintained, such as the streets and roads under the purview of local governments. Yet, as shown in Table 4.9, much of the technology economy infrastructure is privately owned and maintained. In this respect, the deployment of technology economy infrastructure requires public-private negotiations, where local governments like cities provide the access to rights-of-way necessary for technology and telecommunications providers to install technologies—technologies that could benefit the local governments in terms of economic development and their own internal operations.

Not surprisingly, one of the primary sources of tension in the technology economy is conflict between local governments and the private sector concerning the use of public rights-of-way, although the federal Telecommunications Act of 1996 protected the powers of local governments to manage their rights-of-way in reasonable ways (Telecommunications Act of 1996, 1996). Private sector providers want access to the rights-of-way pivotal to the deployment of their technologies, while public sector actors seek to protect these rights-of-way and to allow access in return for desired and targeted investment. One common example of this tension is the digging up of city streets by private sector providers in order to lay fiber-optic cable. Fixing the streets imposes a cost upon the local governments, which then seek to exact some form of compensation in return or up front, as part of the franchise agreements that provide access to the rights-of-way. For example, city governments might charge a fee for access to rights-of-way, require additional fiber-optic cable for city use, negotiate a reduced price for technology services in the city, or negotiate free access for public use (such as schools or public access channels for cable television). City governments might also require that private sector companies provide information about the location and type of infrastructure installed or require that providers deploy the infrastructure in an underserved area. In short, the negotiations over access to and control of rights-of-way is a key point of interaction between the public and private sectors, sometimes resulting in effective public-private partnerships and sometimes resulting in higher costs to one or both sides.

When asked about whether their city governments have control over the rights-of-way in the jurisdiction, 84 percent of economic development officials said yes, compared to 9 percent who said no. In terms of the types of requirements placed on information technology and telecommunications providers, the most common forms cited were franchise fees (87 percent) and access for public use by the city government or schools (64 percent). Requiring additional fiber-optic cable for city use (42 percent) or information about the location and type of infrastructure (35 percent) were also fairly common. Negotiating a reduced

Table 4.10

City Requirements of Rights-of-Way Franchise Agreements ($N = 252$)

	All cities (%)
Franchise fee (such as % of gross receipts)	87
Access for public use (local government, schools, etc.)	64
Additional conduit or fiber-optic cable for city use	42
Information on location and type of infrastructure	35
Reduced price for services	19
Provide service to underserved areas	8

price for technology services (19 percent) or requiring service to be provided to underserved areas (8 percent) were less common (see Table 4.10). Consequently, the regular private market exchange does not help most cities address existing disparities within the city.

Of course, in some instances, cities and other governments do not need to negotiate franchise agreements over rights-of-way because they themselves are directly providing the infrastructure. The public sector can play a direct role in providing or funding certain technologies. For instance, in some states, telecommunications networks may offer increased intermetropolitan or regional fiber-optic bandwidth to the Internet as well as for communications transmission (sometimes referred to as an "Internet backbone") that is publicly funded. When asked whether publicly funded Internet backbones were available in their states, nearly four in ten city economic development officials (38 percent) answered "yes" (24 percent said "no," and 38 percent said "don't know"). Of these economic development officials, 47 percent said that their city utilizes this capacity or connection (30 percent said "no," and 23 percent said "don't know). Often, the rationale for a publicly funded Internet backbone is that the privately provided connections may be located too far away for individual cities to use. When asked how far their cities are from privately operated Internet backbones, economic development officials indicated, on average, a distance of nine miles, ranging from zero (where the backbone is located in or adjacent to the city) to 400 miles away. Some local governments also own telecommunications utilities, although economic development officials indicated that this is less common (6 percent).

One of the reasons why city governments are requiring information about the location and types of infrastructure implemented, public or private, is that there is often a lack of knowledge about existing capacities in cities—knowledge that is necessary for assessing gaps and needs.

Table 4.11

Do Cities Have Inventories of Technology Economy Infrastructure?
(N = 243)

	All cities (%)
Yes	25
No	57
Don't know	18

As recognition of the importance of technology infrastructure has increased in cities, the need for inventorying existing infrastructure and capacity becomes more obvious. Infrastructure inventories are fairly common across more traditional types of infrastructure, such as roads, bridges, ports, or waterways. Similarly, technology infrastructure inventories become a useful tool for cities looking to assess their capacities and needs. As technology applications become available for city use, computer software programs such as Geographic Information Systems offer cities the option of mapping and inventorying infrastructure across the board. Applying this approach to technology economy infrastructure in cities, however, is still a relatively new practice. Even though one-third of economic development officials reported requiring information about the location and type of infrastructure as part of the right-of-way permit process, only one in four (25 percent) said that their cities possessed an inventory of the technology economy infrastructure and its location. Nearly six in ten (57 percent) indicated that their city had no such inventory (see Table 4.11). The results suggest that city governments are not using their right-of-way controls in a beneficial manner. Knowledge of location, type of infrastructure, and capacity would enable cities to target infrastructure development to match business and citizen demands, and would help them identify gaps and areas of greater need that might require city provision of services.

For those cities that have inventories of technology economy infrastructure, economic development officials indicated that the inventories contain incomplete information about location. Two in three economic development officials said that their cities' inventories include fiber-optic cable (69 percent) and wireless towers (66 percent) in the downtown, central business district. The location of wireless towers, in general, was more likely to be included in cities' inventories: three in four economic development officials (74 percent) said that their cities' inventories in-

Table 4.12

Location of Technology Economy Infrastructure in Cities (*N* = 61)
(in percent)

	Downtown CBD*	Industrial or commercial	Office parks	Outlying
Fiber-optic cable	69	61	51	30
Coaxial/hybrid fiber coax	51	51	41	39
Wireless towers	66	74	51	51
Microwave transmitters	26	28	13	13
Satellite facilities	20	15	15	11

*CBD = central business district.

clude wireless towers in industrial or commercial areas, 51 percent said they were in office parks, and 51 percent in outlying areas. Economic development officials also said that inclusion of location information about fiber-optic cable and coaxial/hybrid fiber coax was more likely to be found in their city inventories than was location information about microwave transmitters or satellite facilities (see Table 4.12). Overall, however, location information appears to be spotty and incomplete, a function of the fact that much of this information is privately owned and thus proprietary—a hurdle identified by many city officials, as shown earlier in Table 4.7 (see page 87). For cities that are proactive in collecting infrastructure information, the structure of the information flows, or lack thereof, between the public and private sectors hampers the ability of cities to act in strategic and entrepreneurial ways.

The responses of economic development officials about technology economy infrastructure in cities yield an incomplete picture. Various types of technology economy infrastructure, both wire-line and wireless, are available in many cities. Private sector providers own most of the infrastructure, although cities and others in the public sector could also be providing the infrastructure to some degree. Regardless, the rights-of-way necessary to deploying the infrastructure are controlled by cities and other local governments, which leads to negotiations, and sometimes conflict, between the public and private sectors about access to rights-of-way and franchise agreements. Local demand for technology economy infrastructure places pressure on cities to improve local conditions; however, in many ways cities' abilities to do so are dependent upon their abilities to inventory existing capacity in an effort to identify needs. Most cities have yet to be able to inventory their technology infrastructure, and location information about the infrastructure is particularly difficult to obtain. For city governments and city officials, this picture points to an obvious need for improvement and planning, some of which is under way and highlighted below.

Infrastructure Improvements in Cities

A number of questions emerge when considering improvements that cities are making to better position themselves in the technology economy. What have city governments and other actors in the community been doing to improve their technology economy infrastructure? What types of infrastructure are the focus of these efforts? What are the objectives, or targets, of these investments in terms of economic and community development?

Economic development officials reported considerable movement toward improving technology economy infrastructure in their cities. When asked if their jurisdictions' infrastructure was improved over the past six years (since the passage of the federal Telecommunications Act of 1996[5]) four in five (83 percent) said "yes" and only 4 percent said "no" (the rest saying "don't know"). The key players in making technology economy improvements appear to be private sector telecommunications providers and local governments. Economic development officials indicated that those involved in planning and deploying the infrastructure improvements were primarily telecommunications providers (cited by 87 percent of economic development officials) and local governments (cited by 53 percent). Often, both private and public sector players are simultaneously making improvements in a community's infrastructure, although not necessarily in concert. Four in ten economic development officials (42 percent) said that both private and public sector stakeholders are making improvements, but only 13 percent indicated that improvements were being made through public-private partnerships. In terms of local governments making improvements, the local governments may not necessarily be city or county governments, but might instead be schools. Schools have an obvious stake in technology improvements due to the need to equip students with access and skills, and often are the place of last resort for students without computers and Internet access at home. Economic development officials indicated that schools are involved in making technology improvements about one-third (33 percent) of the time in recent years (see Table 4.13).

Table 4.13

Key Actors in Improving and Deploying Technology Economy Infrastructure (N = 192)

	All cities (%)
Private telecommunications provider(s)	87
Local government	53
Both public and private sectors	42
Schools	33
Other private business	17
Libraries and museums	14
Public-private partnership	13
Nonprofit organizations	4
Neighborhood organizations	1

Table 4.14

Location of Technology Economy Infrastructure Improvements in Cities (N = 252) (in percent)

	Downtown CBD*	Industrial or commercial	Office parks	Outlying
Fiber-optic cable	36	36	26	21
Coaxial/hybrid fiber coax	22	20	16	17
Wireless towers	25	26	19	21
Microwave transmitters	6	5	3	6
Satellite facilities	4	5	3	2

*CBD = central business district.

Most efforts to improve local technology economy infrastructure in recent years appear to be focused around wire-line infrastructure—fiber-optic cable and coaxial/hybrid fiber coax—as well as one type of wireless infrastructure—wireless towers. Other wireless infrastructure, such as microwave transmitters and satellite facilities, are less commonly cited by economic development officials (see Table 4.14). Deployment of the infrastructure also appears to be occurring across the community. Economic development officials pointed to slightly more fiber-optic cable improvements occurring in downtown central business districts (36 percent) and industrial or commercial areas (36 percent) than in office parks (26 percent) or outlying areas in the community (21 percent). Less notable differences were indicated in terms of coaxial/hybrid fiber coax and wireless towers.

Table 4.15

**Objectives of Technology Economy Infrastructure Improvements
(N = 171)**

	All cities (%)
Enhance regional backbone and distribution systems	56
Attract business/jobs	55
Serve special needs like schools, government	46
Attract technology economy businesses	45
Provide service to an underserved area	45
Leverage existing technology economy infrastructure	37
Diversify economic base of city	35
Increase tax revenues	31
Utilize other physical infrastructure (roads, sewer)	22
Redevelopment	21
Downtown revitalizations	20
Telecommuting centers	13
Telecommunications hotels*	9

* Buildings rented to telecommunications tenants to house network equipment.

Cities view the private and sometimes public sector–led technology infrastructure improvements as benefiting both building blocks of the technology economy and the infrastructure itself, as well as attracting technology economy industries. Approximately half of the economic development officials surveyed thought that the objective of the improvements was attracting businesses and jobs to the community (55 percent) or attracting technology economy businesses in particular (45 percent). One in three economic development officials also said that diversifying the economic base of the city (35 percent) and increasing tax revenues (31 percent) were key objectives. On the infrastructure side, about half of economic development officials cited objectives of enhancing the regional telecommunications backbone and distribution systems (56 percent), deploying infrastructure to meet special needs like those of schools or the government itself (46 percent), or providing service to an underserved area (45 percent). Another commonly cited objective was leveraging existing telecommunications infrastructure (37 percent). Some city officials indicated that technology economy infrastructure improvements were tied to other city objectives such as downtown revitalization, redevelopment, or as a means of improving the utilization of other physical infrastructure (see Table 4.15).

Of course, the most oft-cited objective of enhancing the regional telecommunications backbone and distribution system suggests that city officials stress the need for investment in infrastructure networks that go beyond city borders—or that existed outside of city borders and needed to be extended to serve their cities. The response highlights the tension, noted in Chapters 1 and 2, between infrastructure that is often regional in nature and units of government that are typically subregional. This disconnect could translate into competition among jurisdictions for the infrastructure and associated economic benefits or, conversely, could create incentives for jurisdictions to partner around deploying infrastructure to benefit multiple communities in the region. The calculus involved in whether cities view each other as competitors or partners might depend upon how individual cities and their city officials view their infrastructure capacity relative to neighboring jurisdictions. When asked how the technology economy infrastructure in their city compared to neighboring local governments, economic development officials indicated that their infrastructure was more likely to be the same as (55 percent) or better than (34 percent) their neighboring jurisdiction's infrastructure. Only 11 percent of economic development officials said that their infrastructure was worse than that of their neighboring local governments. This sense of being relatively well positioned in the region in terms of technology economy infrastructure capacity may explain the higher likelihood that economic development officials will characterize their neighboring jurisdictions as partners (54 percent) rather than competitors (22 percent) or reluctant collaborators (17 percent).

Responses on regional competitiveness issues suggest that there is considerable opportunity for regional cooperation on the investment in, and deployment of, technology economy infrastructure. Given the regional nature of telecommunications and the leading role of private providers, regional cooperation of local governments may be an untapped source of power and influence over how technology economy infrastructure is deployed. Whether local jurisdictions are in need of better capacity or not, a collective strategy may engender more private interest in serving localities' needs, with collaborative efforts helping private providers identify untapped or underserved markets or reducing private sector costs through economies of scale. The hands-off role of the federal government in the United States in terms of broadband deployment also presents an opportunity for local governments to capitalize on current flexibility and collaborate regionally.

Summary

The Economic Development and Technology Economy Survey offers a view of the perspectives of city economic development officials during a period of time (2002) in which the economy and technology were changing very rapidly. City officials were coping with significant economic and fiscal challenges during this period, a marked departure from the unprecedented growth of the 1990s and early part of the new century. The technology economy–driven boom and bust likely raised questions in the minds of local officials about the role of the technology economy in their own local economic arenas and may have called into question city efforts to invest in technology economy infrastructure. For cities that experienced little technology economy–driven growth during the boom years, the bust might raise concerns about entrenched disparities between those leading and lagging in technology economy growth. In short, the perspectives of city officials during this period were almost certainly influenced by shorter-term changes in the economic system that most likely tempered the optimism often associated with the "go-go '90s."

The perspectives of city economic development officials also formed against a backdrop of longer-term socioeconomic change that may have been slowed to some degree by the economic downturn in 2001, but is still progressing nonetheless. Cities and their local and regional economies are increasingly challenged by longer-term shifts from manufacturing-based, to services-based, to increasingly technology- and information-based economic growth. Globalization, demographic changes, and heightened tensions between state and local governments about the arrangements needed to foster economic growth have accompanied these economic shifts. As local policymakers, scholars, and analysts contemplate the future of local economies, the opinions expressed by local officials should prove helpful in identifying local issues and perceived needs. The key findings and conclusions drawn from the survey results are summarized below.

City officials see their cities as key players in the technology economy. Cities are very involved in the business of economic development writ large, with considerable staffing and resources committed to development efforts. As part of their economic development efforts, there is some understanding and recognition that cities play a dual role with respect to the technology economy, both as economic agents seeking to attract and retain technology economy industry and business and as public sector investors in technology economy infrastructure. In this regard, the definition of the technology economy offered in this book, both as a combination of economic sectors and as key infrastructure, fits well with the local policymaking roles.

City economic development officials see the growth of the technology economy as an essential component in their local economies and as central to the daily operations of their cities. While they view their roles as involving investment in infrastructure and attracting and retaining business, they tend to see their primary role as dealing with the needed infrastructure to attract industry, rather than the other way around, exhibiting an "if we build it, they will come" attitude toward technology economy growth.

Yet, despite these views, few city economic development officials reported that their cities have developed technology economy–focused development plans. In fact, technology economy planning in cities appears to be a relatively recent phenomenon. Those cities that do have plans developed them at some point between 1998 and 2001, and about half of the economic development officials reported that their cities would develop plans in the ensuing couple of years. Current plans are also relatively rudimentary in scope, focusing primarily on promoting cities using city government and economic development websites.

A key barrier to cities' involvement in the technology economy appears to be a lack of knowledge about the technology infrastructure that is already in place. Most economic development officials expressed knowledge about the availability of various types of infrastructure, both wire-line and wireless, within their cities. In most cases, private sector providers—telephone companies, telecommunications companies, and utilities—were identified as the lead providers of the infrastructure, but cities were also identified as playing an active role in deploying the infrastructure. City provision of technology economy infrastructure seems to be mainly focused, to date, on providing improved access to the Internet backbone, given that some economic development officials reported that their cities are located too far away from or have poor connections to existing Internet backbones in the region.

Aside from deploying specific types of infrastructure, cities' main role with respect to all types of infrastructure comes through the control of access to their rights-of-way, regardless of the provider. A large majority of economic development officials reported that their cities control these rights-of-way and that they leverage this control in various ways, through fees, requirements that infrastructure serve schools and government buildings, requirements or incentives to provide the infrastructure in previously underserved areas, or information requirements about the location of infrastructure—yet many economic development officials reported that their cities lack inventories of existing infrastructure. These requirements and cities' use of their control of rights-of-way is one of the main sources of tension between the public and private sectors.

Private sector ownership of existing infrastructure and the interaction with public control of rights-of-way is one barrier to strategic local involvement in the technology economy. Economic development officials also point to a number of other challenges. Chief among these is a lack of funding for targeted efforts, a common barrier to most local government initiatives. Also common is the presence of federal and/or state regulatory controls that preempt or constrict local activities. Several economic development officials also made comments similar to one official's note that "a major barrier is the unwillingness of the private sector to provide the infrastructure." This set of challenges points to a larger collaboration and partnership problem that exists among levels of government and between the public and private sectors. Economic development officials' identification of the barriers to local activity suggests that there is considerably more policy space available for strategically focused cooperation among all of these actors to capitalize on technology economy growth and development. A positive sign in this regard is the view among economic development officials that other nearby cities and jurisdictions are more likely to be potential collaborators rather than competitors. As one economic development official noted, "economic development in this arena needs to be a team effort, with intergovernmental and private collaboration."

In total, the evolutionary picture of cities' roles and activities in the technology economy is very much one of a process in its infant stages—with cities recognizing the need for expanded activities, but embracing a strategy of defining roles, evaluating options, and working toward developing more strategic, long-term planning and policymaking. Chapter 5 seeks to provide further insight and context to cities' roles and activities in the technology economy through case studies of several cities that responded to the survey.

5

Entrepreneurial Cities in the Technology Economy

> The pattern of development of cities today is subject to control, *it is not* the result of uncontrollable forces, *is not* the result of iron economic laws whose effects states are powerless to influence.
>
> —*Peter Marcuse and Ronald van Kempen*

> The overriding public policy need is for leadership in creating a cohesive framework for public and private investment in digital technology systems for communities.
>
> —*Thomas A. Horan*

The technology economy is changing the landscape of local government. As the previous chapters have shown, localities have reasons to not just be aware of these changes but respond to them. Accordingly, the role that local policymakers play in shaping their response to these changes, and the activities that they pursue as a result, are a key part of any description of the technology economy. As expected, all cities are not responding in a common manner because the technology economy has differential effects. Understanding what issues cities are responding to and how cities are crafting their responses is the focal point of this chapter. To this end, I examine entrepreneurial actions in seven cities that are designing planning efforts and strategies with respect to the technology infrastructure and sectors in order to overcome conflict with the private sector or lack of knowledge about their technology infrastructure and their competitiveness at a regional or national level. Each of these cities utilizes its technology infrastructure as an asset, whether it be through creating and maintaining an inventory on the location, capacity, and ownership of all technology infrastructure; incorporating and formulizing a role for technology and telecommunications into economic development planning documents; or using technology infrastructure as a specific policy device. Most cities have crafted a role for technology infrastructure with the intent of positive economic development returns, and in many cases have designed strategies to create, retain, and attract technology sectors appropriate for their economies. Consequently, the collection of these cities' stories demonstrates a holistic policy approach leading to a position of strength in the technology economy.

Traditionally, local economic development policymakers all struggle with the same question: how to use economic development policy to increase the well-being of their local citizens. The trade-offs that accompany this pursuit are many. Should better jobs, more jobs, and/or greater tax collection come at the expense of quality of life? Roger Vaughan's definition of economic development demonstrates a multi-faceted decision: "Economic development is the process of innovation through which we increase the capacity of individuals and organizations to create wealth. The goods and services we value include not only those items that are traded in the marketplace but also less tangible things—the quality of our environment, public security, and other elements that contribute to our sense of well-being" (Vaughan 1984, 2). In shaping policies, local policymakers allocate tax dollars and other resources that will have differential impacts on citizens and local business. How technology economy issues enter into these decisions is often a result of a number of factors: competitiveness, peer pressure, a lack of alternatives, local leadership, business demands, and fiscal health as well as shortfalls, to name a few. Regardless, the roles of technology infrastructure and sectors in local economic development policy are not disengaged from the desire for a livable and prosperous community.

In focusing on a few entrepreneurial cities, I discuss four basic approaches that local governments use to integrate the building blocks of the technology economy into their cities' economic development and planning strategies. The first approach is more global in nature and directly addresses how cities view technology infrastructure relative to economic development strategies. A number of cities position technology infrastructure as a formal objective or key element of their economic development planning documents. These documents are often part of a city's comprehensive plan—the city's official statement concerning future growth and development—which includes policy plans to guide land use, development, housing, environmental impact, and capital facilities budgeting. Some of these elements address technology infrastructure; however, within the economic development plans, local policymakers view technology infrastructure as having an instrumental role in the growth and development of business and citizenry's well-being. In this first approach, technology infrastructure is an overarching concern or guiding principle to economic development in a city.

The second approach is related to the first approach because technology infrastructure has a role in economic development efforts; however, the second approach focuses on how cities utilize technology infrastructure, highlighting specific policy actions. For example, cities can utilize technology and telecommunications infrastructure in targeted capacities, like promoting technology zones or incubators for business and deploying fiber-optic networks for superior telecommunications services in a targeted area, without it being a guiding vision for economic development.

The third approach is also related to economic development efforts, but it is more exclusively tied to certain types of business development—how a city uses technology infrastructure to grow, retain, or attract the other building block of the technology economy, technology sectors. Cities that use this approach perceive a more focused or nuanced role for technology infrastructure, which points to how city leaders think about technology sector business in their local economies.

Finally, the fourth approach that cities use to address the technology economy is through a citywide or neighborhood assessment of technology infrastructure availability and capacity. The creation and maintenance of an inventory on the location, capacity, and ownership of all technology infrastructure serves as a major planning tool and asset for economic development, transportation, public works, and local government's own information technology capacity. The presence of this inventory in a variety of cities indicates how these cities link technology infrastructure to the local economy and to the overall livability of their cities. This can also be said about the other three approaches, to varying degrees, suggesting that technology infrastructure and the technology economy are interwoven in different ways in different cities.

The four approaches are not mutually exclusive. In fact, in cities that are the most entrepreneurial in their approach to the technology economy and economic development, all four approaches are combined—they have economic development that targets the technology economy and benefits the community overall, they employ policies that fit with this strategy, they target sectors and work with the private sector to make sure sectoral strategies are successful, and they map, or inventory, their technology infrastructure to ensure that they know where technology infrastructure is located and where it is needed.

This chapter presents examples of technology economy approaches from seven cities that responded to the Economic Development and Technology Economy Survey detailed in Chapter 4. Although a number of cities revealed use of technology infrastructure in economic development efforts, the cities in this chapter show a range of entrepreneurial efforts and are exemplary because of the level of process and implementation needed to fashion a new vision of economic development in relation to the technology economy. The cities examined are Tacoma, Washington, Lansing, Michigan, San Jose, California, Roanoke, Virginia, Mesa, Arizona, Portland, Oregon, and Charlotte, North Carolina. They are diverse in a number of ways. Table 5.1 provides information on each city with respect to technology economy infrastructure, technology economy industry, as well as traditional socioeconomic characteristics, while presenting how each compares to the average city in the survey.

As in Chapter 3, I use data from the survey as well as secondary sources like the Census of Population and the Economic Census. Table 5.1 demonstrates that the cities are located in different regions of the country and represent a range of population sizes, economic and demographic characteristics, and governmental structure. The cities are not all economically robust. For example, of the seven cities, Lansing and Portland experienced the least employment growth between 1998 and 2001 (0.46 percent and 2.03 percent, respectively), and they lag behind next lowest, Roanoke (4.92 percent), by more than a factor of two for Portland and a factor of ten for Lansing. Most of the cities are not even examples of technology-driven success, even though several seem to have above-average technology sector employment. The variation seen in these cities' technology sector employment is also present in their technology infrastructure. Some of the cities find their high-speed lines, wireless towers, or metropolitan bandwidth to be superior to those of the average city in the survey, but in general, variation in infrastructure exists. For example, Roanoke has above-average metropolitan bandwidth but is below average on every other technology infrastructure measure. The diversity of the seven cities examined here, in terms of the factors shown in Table 5.1, suggests that cities do not necessarily need to be leaders in the technology economy to be entrepreneurial in local policies aimed at capturing the benefits of the technology economy. In examining these seven cities' efforts, I provide an overview of the landscape of technology infrastructure and sectors in terms of the local policymaking environment that other cities are likely to follow.

Table 5.1

Characteristics of Highlighted Cities

	Mean/Mode	Roanoke, VA	Tacoma, WA	Lansing, MI	Charlotte, NC	Mesa, AZ	San Jose, CA	Portland, OR
Technology economy infrastructure								
Telecom strategy usage	Yes	Yes	Yes	Yes	Yes	Yes	Yes	Yes
Deploy fiber	Yes	No	Yes	Yes	No	Yes	Yes	Yes
Technology zones	No	Yes	No	Yes	No	No	Yes	No
Technology incubators	No	Yes	No	Yes	No	No	Yes	No
Smart buildings	No	Yes	No	Yes	No	Yes	Yes	Yes
Telecom improvements	Yes	Yes	Yes	Yes	Yes	Yes	Yes	Yes
Metropolitan bandwidth per capita	0.11	0.21	0.05	0.00	0.10	0.04	0.28	0.07
High-speed lines per 1,000 pop.	0.175	0.009	0.015	0.019	0.004	0.012	0.006	0.006
High-speed lines per square mile	1.12	0.86	2.55	1.66	0.70	0.69	1.85	1.49
Wireless towers per 1,000 pop.	0.095	0.031	0.114	0.084	0.109	0.048	0.019	0.064
Wireless towers per square mile	0.23	0.07	0.44	0.29	0.24	0.15	0.10	0.25
Technology economy industry								
% Technology employers	4.17	2.78	2.48	3.73	5.65	3.77	16.43	5.93
% Technology generators	2.83	2.10	1.59	2.35	3.84	2.42	14.05	4.11
Patents per 1,000 pop.	3.14	2.57	1.07	1.38	1.92	3.52	11.15	3.89
% College graduates	16.28	12.13	13.08	13.78	25.97	14.87	20.84	21.25
Traditional characteristics								
Employment growth rate	7.55	4.92	6.34	0.46	5.56	7.36	7.74	2.03
Median household income	43,600	30,719	37,879	34,833	46,975	42,817	70,243	40,146
Poverty rate	12.14	15.95	15.90	16.86	10.62	8.92	8.82	13.07
Housing affordability rate	0.46	0.47	0.37	0.56	0.42	0.40	0.19	0.32
Population 2000	62,830	94,911	193,556	119,128	540,828	396,375	894,943	529,121
% Black	9.87	26.74	11.24	21.91	32.72	2.52	3.50	6.64

% Age 25–34	10.55	11.44	11.38	13.43	14.33	11.71	13.13	13.63
% Over age 64	13.31	15.83	11.34	9.44	8.57	12.83	7.98	11.06
Violent crime rate	9.96	13.85	13.53	15.56	15.24	9.38	19.73	15.20
Urban area/cluster	UA	UA	UA	UA	UA	UA	UA	UA
Principal city	NPC	PC	PC	PC	PC	PC	PC	PC
Metropolitan/micropolitan	Metro	Metro	Metro	Metro	Metro	Metro	Metro	Metro
Form of government	Council manager	Council manager	Council manager	Mayor council	Council manager	Council manager	Council manager	Commission
General revenue from taxes per capita	446.43	1,204.00	552.00	456.00	418.00	222.00	499.00	638.00
General expenditures per capita	1,034.99	2,654.00	1,342.00	1,323.00	1,061.00	920.00	999.00	1,364.00
Quality of life	Yes	Yes	Yes	Yes	Yes	Yes	Yes	Yes
Climate	No	Yes	No	No	Yes	Yes	Yes	Yes
Parks	Yes	Yes	Yes	No	Yes	Yes	Yes	Yes
Setting	Yes	Yes	Yes	No	No	Yes	No	Yes
Health care	Yes	Yes	No	Yes	No	Yes	No	Yes
Workforce	Yes	Yes	No	Yes	Yes	Yes	Yes	Yes
Quality of schools	Yes	Yes	No	No	Yes	Yes	Yes	Yes

Sources: Employment (U.S. Census Bureau 2001b); patents (Hall, Jaffe, and Trajtenberg 2001); unemployment, incomes, poverty, and housing affordability rate (ratio of median family income to median value of owner-occupied housing), population, college graduates, race, and age categories (U.S. Census Bureau 2000a); crime (U.S. Federal Bureau of Investigation 1999); UA = urban area and UC = urban cluster (U.S. Census Bureau 2000c); NPC = not a principal of the metropolitan or micropolitan statistical area and metropolitan (U.S. Census Bureau 2004); regions (U.S. Census Bureau 2002b); bandwidth (Gorman 2004); high-speed lines (Federal Communications Commission 2002); wireless towers (SpectraSite 2004); remaining variables from survey (Hackler 2002).

Technology Infrastructure and Economic Development Plans

Most local governments recognize the importance of their technology infrastructure; however, it is often lumped in among other core or physical infrastructure such as roads, sewer and water lines, and utilities. Some cities distinguish technology infrastructure, recognizing the important role that communications infrastructure plays in growth and development. Some cities highlight technology infrastructure as an essential piece of their economic development policy, incorporating and formulizing the role of technology and telecommunications into their vision and goals. Three of the seven cities fit the latter description: Tacoma, Lansing, and San Jose. Through the description of each city's vision for technology infrastructure, a local government's needs and focus also become evident.

The Pacific Northwest city of Tacoma bills itself as a wired city, evidenced by a website address of Wiredcityusa.com. The city of almost 200,000 in population is located thirty-four miles southeast of Seattle. Its wired-city reputation is a direct result of the technology infrastructure development associated with its city-owned municipal electric utility, Tacoma Power. In the early 1990s the utility planned to build a fiber-optic network to upgrade and control its substations, but it determined that through this expansion the new network would be capable of offering a wide range of telecommunications services within Tacoma city limits. The upgrades resulted in both a hybrid fiber coaxial network and carrier grade fiber network. As of November 1998 Tacoma Power authorized various partnerships with private providers, allowing them to lease their connections and capacity from the "Click! Network" in order to offer residents and businesses of Tacoma cable TV and high-speed Internet broadband services. In addition, businesses can purchase higher-speed services and capacity (Click! Network Tacoma Power 2004).

The Click! Network, a major technology infrastructure project for Tacoma Power and the city, is indicative of the level of interest and commitment that Tacoma has with respect to technology infrastructure. The older northwestern port city has mainly been the homestead for manufacturing industries. Gazing often to the northeast, Tacoma hopes to capture some of the growth that the Seattle area has garnered since the rise of Microsoft and its multitude of spinoffs. The economic vision of Tacoma states that by leveraging the Click! Network investment, the city "has improved the quality of life in the city and established a broadband infrastructure servicing businesses and residents" (Tacoma Economic Development Department 2001, 40). The primary goal for Tacoma centered on its prior and continued investment to provide the "best possible broadband access to business and residents at affordable prices" (Tacoma Economic Development Department 2001, iii). Tacoma's technology infrastructure is directly tied to the economic development goals for the city, and the economic development plan calls for continual monitoring of this investment. The utility and the city conduct a series of affordability and performance benchmarks for the Click! Network operation and services in order to ensure that it is consistent with industry standards and demand. To assess demand, the city works with private providers to determine whether the level of technology infrastructure investment meets the needs of local businesses and is nationally competitive.

Tacoma's vision for technology infrastructure culminates in a number of direct and indirect policy actions, some of which I address in sections on other approaches to technology infrastructure below. However, what makes Tacoma different is the level of importance and priority that the city places on technology infrastructure in its overall strategy for growth and development. The city's economic development visions and goals are set to guide city efforts in future years. Tacoma revisits this vision approximately every five to six years. The current plan, adopted in late 2001, serves as the foundation and suggests that Tacoma realizes that the technology economy is essential to the city's economic vitality.

The critical role that technology infrastructure plays also fits well with Tacoma's overall vision in its comprehensive plan, which is to "serve local investment by keeping pace with infrastructure and capital facility improvements" (Tacoma Economic Development Department 2001, 41). The municipal utility upgrades provided Tacoma with the opportunity to become a city with a superior technology infrastructure, providing residents and businesses with telecommunications services that were beyond what they would have received in 1998 and leaving the city in an advantageous position today.

Tacoma's technology-based vision demonstrates a desire to be more like its large neighbor city, Seattle. Tacoma's port and manufacturing reputation could have led to slower deployment of technology infrastructure in its city limits and would have most certainly not resulted in the level of coverage that the city now possesses. While not all cities are able to draw upon a municipally owned utility to deploy technology infrastructure, Tacoma's strategic use and leveraging of its assets is noteworthy. The city's continual dedication to the success and development of the Click! Network through further investment demonstrates the longevity of technology infrastructure to economic development in Tacoma.

While the city examples presented in this chapter do not all possess the same set of assets, each city has designed an economic development strategy for technology infrastructure that is similar to Tacoma's.

Lansing is in a more challenging position than Tacoma. Although it is the state capital of Michigan, it is also an aging urban core city and its technology infrastructure reflects this status. Over the past two decades, Lansing has suffered from the decline of the automobile industry and two state government workforce policy changes that have undermined the economic base of the city, and in particular the office and commercial lifeblood of Lansing's downtown. The first state workforce policy shift was the outsourcing of various government functions, once conducted in Lansing, to private contractors in Massachusetts and Colorado. The second policy change was the relocation of state employees to private office buildings outside of Lansing's Washington Square corridor, a tax increment finance (TIF) district. The TIF district subsequently lost tax income, and the city lost sales and property tax revenues due to less commercial and retail activity. On the surface, technology economy issues would seem of minor concern in comparison, but Lansing is included in this analysis because of the entrepreneurial spirit of the city's previous mayor, David Hollister. In 2001, Hollister sought to change the economic outlook of Lansing through technology. Like the municipal utility of Tacoma, Hollister provided the motivation and direction to examine the relationship between economic development and technology infrastructure in the city. Announced as the Mayor's Information Technology (IT) Initiative, the city's strategy emerged during a period of time when local governments, including Lansing, were fiscally stable and very much aware of the technology boom that was driving the national economy.

Lansing's IT Initiative sought to understand how IT related to Lansing's citizens and business community and how Lansing could establish itself as a technology leader in the region. The initiative included the assembly of a Lansing IT Assessment Task Force, which evaluated the city's readiness for the "networked world" with the support and participation of Lansing's Economic Development Corporation and the Tax

Increment Finance Authority. The city conducted an "IT Digital Readiness Assessment." This assessment included two forums held among local leaders and stakeholders during which the participants addressed the strengths, weaknesses, opportunities, and constraints in achieving digital readiness. Based on the assessment, Lansing leaders created an overarching vision to guide economic development activities: "Lansing is an economically diverse city that provides education and training opportunities for every person to ensure that the benefits of technology are realized by the entire city" (City of Lansing 2001, 6). Using the vision to guide policy, the task force and city leaders focused on key segments of society (government, schools, business, quality of life, and citizens) to formulate an "e-conomic development plan" in which technology was a focal point (specific policies of the initiative are discussed in the sections to follow).

Today, the IT Initiative continues to guide Lansing's economic development activities, but the initiative has suffered a number of setbacks. First and foremost, the economic recession created and continues to create large budget deficits (nearly $7 million in 2005), generating an atmosphere of workforce reductions and spending cuts across city programs. Second, in January of 2003, the leader of the initiative, Mayor David Hollister, resigned to lead the state of Michigan's newly reorganized State Department of Labor, Economic Growth, and Urban Development. Interim Mayor Tony Benavides pledged continued support, but the mayoral election of 2005 ushered in a new mayor, Virg Bernero. While Mayor Bernero created a taskforce to examine infrastructure and information technology, changing leadership is unlikely to stabilize the initiative. Lansing's experience points to the importance of city leadership to sustain technology-centered economic development initiatives.

The city of San Jose also integrates technology infrastructure into its economic development planning documents. San Jose is in the heart of the Silicon Valley and promotes itself as a high-tech capital through multiple messages and visions. It is not surprising that technology infrastructure is part of San Jose's overall strategy. However, given its privileged location in the midst of a technology hub in the world economy, San Jose might have taken the relationship between technology infrastructure and economic development for granted. In fact, some city officials in widely recognized technology centers claim they do not need to do much since the private market will come to the area based on the demand alone. San Jose, instead, has taken the position that its locational advantages must be nurtured. The city's goals broaden the application of technology infrastructure to a wider audience with their vision of being a "tech savvy city that uses and showcases technology to improve daily life" (Office of City Manager and Office of Economic Development 2003, 16). Tacoma and Lansing each had a motivating agency or leader to focus their attention on technology infrastructure in their goals for economic development and growth. San Jose's motivation is a result of its advantaged position in the technology geography, but it does not want to lose its position as a leading city in the technology economy. More recently, the negative effects of the technology and dot.com bust, with over 92,000 jobs lost in the San Jose metropolitan area alone, has prompted San Jose to capitalize on its assets of global business and reputed technology geography for the sake of economic recovery. San Jose's economic development strategy with respect to technology infrastructure plays out in a number of policies that I address in the sections below.

Tacoma, Lansing, and San Jose are unique in that technology infrastructure plays a strong role in shaping the vision for economic development of each of them. As with any vision, the impetus behind this result provides insight into the manner of their policymaking in the technology economy. In each city an opportunity presented itself. In Tacoma, a desire to capture some of the benefit of its proximity to Seattle and, specifically, the upgrading of Tacoma Power's network suggested that entrepreneurial actions could spill over beyond utilities into economic development. Lansing's entrepreneurial leadership prioritized technology infrastructure as a necessary economic development component to forge a new economic direction for the city. And finally, for San Jose, the city's desire to maintain its position relative to other technology economy competitors resulted in a natural partnership between technology infrastructure and economic development. As cities reflect on the implications of the technology economy for their futures, capturing these opportunities in technology infrastructure may provide a foundation for economic growth. Each of the other cities from which examples are drawn in this chapter distinctly utilizes technology infrastructure in a less strategic, more functionally narrow role.

The remainder of this chapter focuses on three specific approaches that are often, but not always, related to economic development: specific and limited technology policies and strategies, positioning technology infrastructure relative to retention and recruitment of technology business, and finally, assessment and inventorying of local technology infrastructure.

Technology Infrastructure Policies

Technology infrastructure policies are those that carry a specific policy action focused on a particular component of technology infrastructure. Cities that integrate technology infrastructure into their economic development plans as a broader vision or strategy often outline a number of policy actions related to the deployment or development of technology infrastructure. Some cities, however, only have a component, or a few components, of technology infrastructure as specific policy objectives. This section examines the technology infrastructure policies of six cities: Roanoke, Lansing, Mesa, Tacoma, San Jose, and Portland. Although some of the policy actions may seem less novel, others represent entrepreneurial approaches to technology infrastructure in economic development.

Roanoke is the smallest city in this examination of entrepreneurial technology infrastructure policies; however, the range of its approaches is anything but small. It is located about 150 miles east of Richmond, works cooperatively with surrounding counties, cities, and towns as a metropolitan area known as the New Century Region. The city also has its own economic development department that addresses technology infrastructure through a variety of policies. Working to transition its economy during the 1990s from a manufacturing base, Roanoke targeted industries such as biotechnology, optics, information technology and software, and transportation-related manufacturing and services. To facilitate this objective, the city developed and implemented a Technology Initiative in 2001 that included the development of a Technology Zone and redevelopment of Warehouse Row to ready it for technology businesses, as well as providing information on the location and capacity of fiber-optic cable and WiFi networks on the department's website.

After the approval of recommendations, guidelines, and incentives, the city recently had its first technology business locate in its Technology Zone, a zone that encompasses the downtown area and a stretch of land near one of the city's primary transportation connections, Interstate 581. To receive incentives and be able to locate in the zone, qualifying businesses must be engaged in research, design, development, or manufacture of commodities, services, or solutions used in factory automation, biotechnology, chemicals, computer hardware, computer software, computer systems, defense, energy, environmental, manufacturing equipment, medical materials, pharmaceuticals, photonics, subassemblies and components, testing and measurement, telecommunications, and transportation. In addition, qualifying businesses must increase the average number of full-time jobs by at least 10 percent and make a new capital investment of at least $30,000, resulting in an increase of at least 20 percent in assessed value of the firm's real estate and/or in the cost of its personal property. In exchange, businesses would be eligible to receive grants to pay for 50 percent of the costs of extending telecommunication services to their location as well as cover 50 percent of the net increase in taxes (business personal property and real estate taxes) from the capital investment (Roanoke Economic Development 2005).

To facilitate Roanoke's Technology Zone, the city took a number of steps to ready the technology infrastructure and real estate, concentrating on the redevelopment of the downtown area, dubbed Roanoke's e-Town. As a result of a public-private partnership, Roanoke has had a free wireless Internet zone (WiFi) downtown since 2003.[1] The city recently expanded the WiFi network to increase coverage in the downtown area as well as reach the main public library. In addition, the city redeveloped warehouses into smart building space (Warehouse Row Business Center) in order to provide wired office space for technology companies. Finally, these projects are supported through the department's Wired for Business website. The pages provide information on the Technology Zone, e-Town, the WiFi Network, as well as fiber-optic cable maps for the region, city, downtown area, and in the Technology Zone. Roanoke's Department of Transportation created these maps and helps maintain them to keep economic development abreast of any changes with privately financed renovation of buildings in the city. Roanoke combined a number of policy actions using various aspects of technology infrastructure to create a new environment capable of supporting the city's desired growth. The Technology Initiative and its strategies are central to Roanoke's recruitment of targeted business into a redevelopment zone. The city's partnership to provide free wireless broadband and its role as an information disseminator of telecommunications options in the city and region point to the city's commitment to the interdependence of technology infrastructure and future economic development growth.

Lansing's IT Initiative included a number of goals that had broader effects than economic development, like e-government and educational training programs for schools, families, and nonprofit organizations. Yet the initiative's central vision guided the creation of the e-conomic development plan. The plan outlined the city's desire for technology infrastructure and how this related to the attraction, growth, and retention of IT-based businesses. The city sought to develop a technology infrastructure plan that included a phased approach to ensure high-speed affordable Internet at various price ranges. To facilitate this objective, the city envisioned that an assessment of all telecommunications infrastructure demand and supply would be essential. The mapping of the infrastructure could allow the city to understand current capacity and plan for future needs, but the analysis of demand and forecasting of usage by different types of business, organizations, schools, and libraries, as well as government entities, could provide a clearer picture of the city's readiness for change. The city partnered with the Lansing Board of Water and Light, the municipal utility provider, and other service providers, like Ameritech, to map fiber-optic cable and DSL infrastructure. For the demand assessment and greater mapping of other wireless and hybrid fiber coaxial cable infrastructure, the city participated in the analysis conducted by the Regional Economic Development Team for the counties of Ingham (containing Lansing), Eaton, and Clinton under the state's Link Michigan program of the Michigan Economic Development Corporation (Regional Economic Development Team 2003). The analysis indicated that Lansing was second only to Detroit in the level of technology infrastructure connectivity, but that this infrastructure was aging and had little capacity to serve increased and more sophisticated access. In addition, there was a lack of public awareness of technology and benefits of computerization among both businesses and residents.

With this information, the city set out to examine how it could provide policies and incentives to provide a more digitally ready Lansing, from educating businesses on the benefits of available technology to working with private real estate providers to educate them on the importance of building readiness, or smart buildings. The city's outreach efforts resulted in collaboration with the Lansing Regional Chamber of Commerce, supporting both its TechConnect Program, which promotes the increased use of technology and technical services by businesses, and its Small Business Services division.

The city continues to hold educational and stakeholder forums to evaluate the IT Initiative's goals. In June of 2004, "Destination Cool: Visioning Lansing's Technology Future" brought technology end users, service providers, public officials, and economic development professionals together to discuss Lansing's current trends and challenges in technology and broadband use. Although the forum highlighted a number of topics and critical needs, participants expressed that the government's presence is needed to support the implementation of technology infrastructure through the provision of incentives and removal of regulatory barriers (similar to those provided to the manufacturing sector) and to provide current technology infrastructure maps. From the city leaders' perspectives, the economic recession has slowed much of the progress on the deployment of technology infrastructure. However, a few local private service providers are continuing to facilitate working toward technology infrastructure goals. One participant in the IT Initiative forums and Destination Cool conference is in the process of deploying a high-speed wireless network throughout downtown Lansing. While there is a broader economic development strategy for technology infrastructure in Lansing, as outlined in the previous section, the strategy is made tangible through a variety of technology-centered policies, as described here.

The city of Mesa, twenty miles east of Phoenix, is located in one of the nation's fastest-growing metropolitan areas. As the fortieth largest U.S. city by population, Mesa adopted two programs in 2000 that strongly influence its economic development efforts around technology infrastructure—E-Streets and Connecting Mesa. Both programs support the economic development goal of creating comprehensive transportation, communication, and infrastructure systems to ensure movement of commerce and information. The two programs are the outcome of the city's inability to land a major corporation's data center in 1999, a result attributed to the city's lack of telecommunications infrastructure. In response, the city, with the assistance of stakeholders from business, communications services, education, and real estate development, conducted an assessment of its infrastructure to benchmark Mesa's connectedness in 2000. The city utilized an established assessment tool and was the first city in the state of Arizona to undergo such a self-evaluation. The overarching product of the process was an inventory of technology infrastructure—mapping of fiber-optic lines, wireless networks, DSL and cable modems. Although the city seemed to have adequate fiber-optic lines, only 20 percent of residential homes were able to receive high-speed services. In addition, the city realized that each of the key stakeholders had a role in this technology infrastructure problem and the connections to economic development: (1) the real estate industry could improve the planning and wiring of office and homes; (2) residential access needed improvement to nurture the flexibility of working from home; (3) businesses desired greater access to e-government services like online permitting; and (4) small businesses were in need of training and education programs to understand how to utilize technology (Mesa Electronic Streets Task Force 2000).

Connecting Mesa emerged from these latter realizations, resulting in specific programs to address education of students, residents, and small businesses in technology usage, workforce development, and wired real estate. Although each program addressed economic development concerns, the city chose another route to directly address the state of technology infrastructure in Mesa. The city created the Electronic Streets (E-Streets) Initiative "to aid the work of the private sector that is necessary to support the construction of robust community-wide broadband telecommunication networks for use by the community" (Mesa E-Streets and Licensing Broadband Development Office 2004b). The city placed the initiative under the direction of the E-Streets and Licensing Broadband Development Office in Mesa's Department of Financial Services. The office "advocates for and protects the public interest in the regulation and development of broadband telecommunications and cable communications systems, which make use of the public rights-of-way within the City of Mesa, and monitors and helps resolve subscribers' concerns" (Mesa E-Streets and Licensing Broadband Development Office 2004b).

The technology infrastructure focus of the initiative complemented the existing activities of this office. For example, through the licensing process, the office maintains knowledge of the location and capacity of all available telecommunications infrastructure in the 175-square-mile city. However, the E-Streets Initiative goes beyond licensing. The city leverages the deployment of its own networks in an entrepreneurial venture to increase broadband networks in the city. The city has constructed over thirty-five miles of in-road trenches or duct banks, and each of the E-Streets duct banks includes twelve conduits, the pipes that are necessary to protect fiber-optic cable networks in any trench deployment (Mesa E-Streets and Licensing Broadband Development Office 2004a). The city maintains four of the conduits for its own institutional fiber-optic network to provide the network facilities for fire, police, and utility services as well as traffic surveillance in the growing city. The remaining eight empty conduits are available for commercial sale and provided to interested parties at the lowest practical cost. Mesa views this venture as a way to entice infrastructure investment, but the city remains free of maintenance and operation of all private networks in the trenches beyond the city-designated conduits that provide only city services. Each telecommunications service provider must maintain and repair its respective conduit and network.

The economic development office's comprehensive infrastructure strategy calls for the continuation of E-Streets Initiative and stresses its importance to the facilitation of new telecommunications and information technology applications in the city. In addition, E-Streets' construction of the city's network is flexible with economic development priorities. With advance planning, the network provided fiber-optic spurs off of the main loop architecture to several economic development projects (Ellsworth, Queen Creek, Williams Gateway, Arizona Health Park, and Falcon Drive). The network also has several extensions to accommodate other city needs like a sewer interceptor project, fire stations, and traffic coordination. The cost of extending while the roads are torn up and the trenches are open is much less than with new construction at a separate time.

Mesa's E-Streets trench venture spills over into other licensing activities in the office. When a telecommunications provider wants to deploy more telecommunications infrastructure on city-owned property, the provider must receive a permit or license because the construction will occur in an area that is under Mesa's rights-of-way. The E-Streets Office negotiates these licenses and is often able to receive extra services from the granting of the license. For example, a recent negotiation provided the city with 1.7 miles of fiber-optic cable for $100,000 instead of the market price tag of $300,000 to 400,000 if the city built the span itself. Mesa's approach to technology infrastructure is as direct as possible without building the infrastructure and providing it directly to business and residents. The leveraging of existing projects, both public and private, shows Mesa's entrepreneurial capacity in addressing an earlier lost opportunity.

The city of Tacoma has the municipal electric utility advantage, and the economic development efforts of the city have embraced this relative advantage to implement a number of technology infrastructure policies. With regard to the city's growth management, economic development impacts and analysis address all infrastructure, capital improvements, transportation, and land-use issues, not unlike other cities. However, for Tacoma all growth management plans address the question of whether the city's technology network should be extended. This is particularly true in the case of all new private developments and buildings, where the city considers whether it is possible to connect all new developments to the Click! Network. City leaders believe that in leveraging private investments, the city receives the best return on public infrastructure investment. As a side benefit, such expansions will increase the longevity and sustainability of the Click! Network. This approach is also applied to redevelopment projects. For example, network expansion is part of the city's strategy to improve older city assets like the Port of Tacoma. In a partnership with the Port of Tacoma, the city is seeking to expand broadband facilities to the port to support the growth in marine traffic and improvement in communications between other countries and the port (Tacoma Economic Development Department 2001).

The city of San Jose has a number of technology infrastructure–focused policies. As one of the first cities in the United States to offer a free wireless network in its downtown in the area around pedestrian-friendly San Pedro Square and its convention center, the city is currently looking to expand the network. The city has hired a private consultant to benchmark what other cities are doing in WiFi and gather stakeholder input through a series of focus groups to determine what the uses of additional capacity could be in libraries, parks, recreation centers, and at the airport. City municipal workers, neighborhood business associations, opinion leaders, and local service providers will offer ideas about possible uses, such as parking meters, traffic surveillance, and water and other utility meter reading. The exercise will determine the feasibility of the wireless network before tax dollars are spent. This process comes on the heels of San Jose having already reached its goal of 100 percent broadband service coverage (cable modems and DSL). Although mainly a private market phenomenon, the city prompted and monitored the progress of service providers like SBC and Comcast attaining this wired community feat.

Finally, Portland is a city that is just beginning to recognize the importance of technology infrastructure to its economic development potential. Although this Pacific Northwest city has a reputation for both high-technology and bioscience industry, until recently Portland had not considered the development of technology infrastructure as an important part of its environment. In 2002, the mayor appointed a Blue Ribbon Committee to develop the city's second economic development plan.

Under the guidance of the Portland Development Commission, a comprehensive economic development strategy declared that the city did not have "a clear strategy to support the development or the expansion of telecommunications infrastructure essential to accommodate today's business operations" (Portland Development Commission 2002a, 8). Seeing this as a serious problem to facilitating the redevelopment of Portland's industrial base, the plan laid out a strategy for telecommunications that included support for the expansion of a state-of-the-art communications technology for Portland business.

Portland worked with private sector providers to ensure that infrastructure was present and services could be provided. The result was the development of Unwire Portland, a project designed to provide high-capacity bandwidth to buildings, retain and expand the opportunity for creative and high-technology services, and improve broadband services for local residents. Unwire Portland will be a wireless network developed by a selected private telecommunications provider. The Portland Telecommunications Steering Committee will define requirements of the network, which will be financed, built, and managed by the private company; Portland will be an "anchor tenant." As the largest customer of the network, the city plans on using it for various government services, public safety, and providing Internet service to riders of TriMet, Portland's public transit. The city believes that the wireless network will lower city telecommunications expenses and encourage competition (Portland Development Commission 2005). The city disseminated a request for proposals in September of 2005 so that private providers could bid for the project; in April of 2006 Portland selected MetroFi Inc., a wireless network provider headquartered in Mountain View, California, to deliver and operate a citywide WiFi network. The project participants envision that the network services will be available by the end of 2007. The city views this technology infrastructure strategy as providing a foundation for Portland's future while lessening the present gaps in Portland's existing infrastructure.

Each of the cities highlighted in this section has made efforts to offer technology infrastructure as a specific policy device or action in hopes of generating economic growth and development. Although the cities' policies vary from more narrow ones looking at specific infrastructure projects or for specific industries, to broader effects on business and residents through wireless networks, technology infrastructure is seen as a key policy component in economic development efforts.

Recruiting Technology Sectors
with Technology Infrastructure

Thus far, the review of how cities are employing technology infrastructure within economic development plans has focused on the efforts to utilize technology infrastructure in a more generalized and overarching manner—from it being a foundation upon which cities design their visions and goals for economic development to specific policy actions related to the deployment or development of technology infrastructure to attain economic development objectives. All of the cities discussed above also craft a role for technology infrastructure with the intent of creating, retaining, and/or attracting technology sectors appropriate for their economies, often referred to as high-tech or IT (see Chapter 2). As found in Chapter 3, telecommunications infrastructure in aggregate has a positive effect on a city's employment in technology sectors. Local physical technology infrastructure is more likely to affect technology employers while local policies and strategies that integrate infrastructure into economic development plans are more likely to affect technology generators. Understanding how cities create and structure such policies is essential for understanding the technology economy, as well as for providing an awareness of what is viable for local economic development practitioners seeking to partake in the technology economy.

The city of Roanoke refers to its economic development strategy as "three legs of a stool," with the city concentrating on development of tourism, industry, and biotechnology. The city expanded on the biotechnology leg in its "Vision 2001 2020," seeking to target a number of sectors under a strategic initiative, but noting that the new economic initiatives would require a shifting of gears for the city. The initiative sought to develop a new economic base for the city through the development and implementation of an economic development strategy that attracts, retains, and expands businesses in biotechnology, optics, and information technology/software. In the process, the city recognized that this strategic change would require investment in the critical amenities of education, land use, environment, and recreation to provide the high quality necessary to attract the desired industries. "Roanoke must attract knowledge-based industries by having a pool of qualified workers, a research and development presence, telecommunications infrastructure, transportation services (air and rail service), water quality, non-interruptible power, and a high quality of life" (Roanoke 2001, 57).

To develop this new base of technology industries, the city prioritized technology infrastructure that would have the most supportive effect. To begin with, the city approached all normal in-road utility improvements in a strategic manner, installing extra conduit for future use and sale. This strategy, not unlike Mesa's joint trench venture, reduces the overall cost of future fiber-optic network deployments because it lessens the impact on the city's roads. With conduit available, the city's rights-of-way will be under less stress from future requests of telecommunications providers because more of these networks can be deployed without additional construction; this works to increase the road infrastructure's life while reducing citizen complaints about the inconvenience of road closures.

The city also has a number of indirect technology infrastructure programs to support technology sector development. For example, through Roanoke's e-Town initiative, the Warehouse Row Business Center was completed and fully leased to technology companies requiring flexible, wired office space; the city also established the previously mentioned Technology Zone, in which technology infrastructure is a benefit and an enticement to businesses looking for a location. In addition, the city has two industrial parks. The first, the Roanoke Centre for Industry and Technology, is a 440-acre park that the city acquired, developed, and marketed in its local enterprise zone. The city's other venture is with Roanoke's Redevelopment and Housing Authority and the Carilion Roanoke Memorial Hospital. The resulting Riverside Centre for Research and Technology is a plan for a new 100-acre business park that is only recently under way. In 2005, the public-private partnership broke ground for the Carilion Biomedical Institute. The Institute already has a number of innovation-oriented companies signed on as new residents (American Biosystems, Medical Enzymatics, and Luna Innovations); in addition, the presence of Carilion has resulted in Roanoke's being home to three other biomedical companies (PhysioAdvantage, Surgical Tools, and Zpro) through various early-stage partnerships. Whether through direct or indirect investment, public-private partnerships in Roanoke help the city achieve its goal of attracting technology businesses with a diverse and strategic balance of technology infrastructure policies to provide the necessary infrastructure.

San Jose has a similar approach to attracting technology sector companies with indirect and public-private-focused approaches to investing in technology infrastructure. Through several strategic partnerships with

San Jose State University, the city created the Bioscience Incubator and Innovation Center. Located in the Edenvale Technology Park, the incubator and center opened in late 2004 and includes 2,312 acres, with 8 million square feet of research and development, office, and manufacturing space. The incubator provides a number of services normally found in such spaces like start-up assistance programs, support services, educational and mentoring services, networking opportunities, technology transfer services, commercialization services, and links to investment and venture capital funds. The city also has incubators serving smaller, new technologically-oriented environmental products and software companies in the environmental and software business clusters. In both Roanoke's and San Jose's technology parks and incubators, the cities ensure that the spaces are able to meet the functional telecommunications and other technology infrastructure requirements of the targeted technology companies as well as supply various small company needs.

Mesa's economic development office looks to entrepreneurial and small businesses for technology economy growth. The city works to maintain relationships with technology businesses through roundtables and other city-sponsored networking opportunities in order to understand their needs. During a recent mayoral roundtable, one technology company owner reported that employees regularly complained about its Mesa location, voicing concern about the city's conservative, religious, homogeneous reputation in comparison to Tempe's young population and university-centered entertainment and nightlife. The city has used this and other feedback to develop a long-term plan to address this problem, mainly through renovation of its downtown. Mesa is opening a new $95 million arts center and creating a community college campus downtown. However, the desires of these companies do not stop at quality-of-life amenities. The downtown area also suffered from a lack of technology infrastructure. Through Mesa's self-assessment and mapping of infrastructure, the city created an open channel for communication between local telecommunications providers and the city in terms of technology services for business and citizens. The city held meetings with telecommunications providers to show where the city's technology infrastructure was not meeting business needs, and this information influenced the capital improvement plans of telecommunications providers, as some providers shifted resources to areas with greater need. When the city reevaluated their technology infrastructure, they found that coverage had expanded substantially, but noted that this was also due to the surge in investment during the telecommunications boom in the late 1990s and early part of 2000–2001.

However, other employment areas suitable to technology industry in Mesa also lacked infrastructure. E-Streets' East Loop project is one example of how Mesa is trying to utilize technology infrastructure to assist with technology sector development. With more than twenty miles of the thirty-five-mile loop completed and fourteen slated for construction this year, the finished loop will connect Falcon Field, a general aviation airport, to Williams Gateway, a former U.S. Air Force base. This construction over the past three years has been important to the growth and retention of business in the area. For example, Falcon Field is home to Boeing's Apache helicopter production facility as well as MD Helicopters, formerly McDonnell Douglas, a production facility for the Model 500 series military helicopters. The construction of the city's telecommunications network in this East Loop extended city services to the area as well as affording a number of service providers the opportunity through the E-Streets' joint trench venture to become a provider at a lower cost than if they constructed their own networks. The project has assisted in the growth of aviation support and spillover businesses as well as other services in the area.

The strategy in Mesa suggests that the city views the private sector as the leader in defining technology infrastructure needs, but the city government makes policies and choices about the infrastructure (usually in response to private sector needs). The city's self-assessment and its creation of the E-Streets trench venture program are two examples of Mesa's approach to technology infrastructure investment.

The city of Tacoma, on the other hand, finds itself in a very different position as the owner of the fiber-optic network of Tacoma Power. The city utilizes this technology asset to attract and grow advanced technology industry, especially emerging computer-related business. The city addresses the development of this industry through financial incentives, land use and zoning, and direct technology infrastructure planning. For example, Tacoma does not require Internet service providers to pay a business and occupation tax (a common form of business taxation in cities in the state of Washington). The city also monitors the amount of built space and developable land available to accommodate the needs of advanced technology companies. This includes the consideration of innovative zoning and site assembly for larger campus sites (Tacoma Economic Development Department 2001). Each of these actions includes a role for technology infrastructure. The city maintains maps of the location of high-speed fiber connections, working to ensure that a majority of privately-owned and -developed buildings are served by fiber. The city reviews the technology infrastructure needs of companies and targets city resources to address shortcomings, whether through leveraging the existing municipal utility network or working with private telecommunications providers. In general, the city seeks to understand what technology companies consider to be the area's advantage or disadvantage when contemplating a move to Tacoma or choosing to leave. Knowledge of how technology infrastructure fits with respect to other location factors is a priority for Tacoma's technology sector efforts.

Portland's foray into Unwire Portland is also, to some degree, driven by the desire for a vibrant technology sector. Portland's Blue Ribbon Commission report recognized the importance of several factors for the growth and expansion of technology industries. The commission's findings noted the importance of building space with high-speed lines and recognized that the success of the Pearl District (a now-prospering commercial and residential sector on the east side of the city's downtown) with dot.com growth during 2000 and 2001 was a result of technology renovation (Portland Development Commission 2002b). At this point in time, the Unwire Portland initiative is in an incubating phase because the city hopes it will create a technology infrastructure platform for entrepreneurs, high-bandwidth office buildings, and a marketing buzz about Portland being a technologically savvy city.

The analysis of technology infrastructure vis-à-vis technology sector development in the cities examined above demonstrates the versatility of technology infrastructure policy options. The desire for a growing technology sector is met by both direct and indirect investments in technology infrastructure development, from provision of capacity to creating suitable technology spaces in incubators and smart buildings. The feature that all of these cities share is a strong emphasis on public-private partnerships, in terms of identifying the needs of targeted businesses and sectors and in working with private sector technology providers to develop and implement plans for technology infrastructure investment.

These strategies, however, are not necessarily limited in capacity to influencing a narrow sector. Strategies for technology infrastructure investment tend to act as an enabling force. The benefits of the investment often disperse beyond just the recruited firm. Most of the cities discussed in this section are approaching technology infrastructure in an entrepreneurial manner. Cities see the connection to economic growth and seek to exploit it through strategic investments that leverage public and private investment and are based on assessments of public and private needs.

Technology Infrastructure Inventories

The fourth approach in terms of city strategies in the technology economy deals with how cities utilize technology infrastructure inventories and assessments, some of which has been addressed through the description of the other three approaches. The majority of cities that are creating and maintaining inventories of the location, capacity, and ownership of technology infrastructure do so to serve three general functions. The first is related to economic development attraction, growth, and retention programs, where economic development policymakers use the information to ensure that buildings or developable lands meet the functional telecommunications requirements of business prospects looking to relocate or expand in the city. Second, in some cities the department of transportation or planning keeps an inventory of all private telecommunications deployments in order to strictly manage a city's rights-of-way, limiting chaos and costs associated with multiple network deployments and construction in and below city streets. The third function is also related to rights-of-way management, but instead of transportation coordination, the inventory serves as the foundation for licenses and franchises through which the city negotiates for some extra functionality, whether it is collected fees, joint venture opportunities, or additional infrastructure for schools, underserved areas, and/or public spaces.

Although identifying each type of inventory provides background on the project, the uses of these inventories quickly blur departmental boundaries in city governments. This is not unexpected, and actually local government agencies should not isolate such entrepreneurial collections of information. Indeed, of the cities with inventories of technology infrastructure, most have found a number of strategic uses beyond the impetus behind the original collection of information. Cities that use the inventory information in multiple ways have noted that their inventories influence other planning and policy activities, which in turn increases interdepartmental support for timely updating of their infrastructure inventory. Just as the benefits of technology infrastructure policies for technology sector development disperse, so do the benefits of inventories.

Inventories and Economic Development

The preceding sections examined technology infrastructure as it relates directly to the economic development efforts of cities. Several of the cities sought to understand what the locality had to offer in terms of technology infrastructure for business and its citizens. Often the self-evaluation process or assessment of technology infrastructure came as part of a new technology economy strategy. Lansing's IT Initiative is a perfect example. As part of the city's desire to bring affordable broadband to business and citizens, in 2002 the city's Infrastructure Subcommittee began to inventory Lansing's existing information technology infrastructure and services, including hardware such as computers and broadband components and providers of technology services (Lansing Economic Development Corporation 2003). The city wanted to map all types of users, from business and nonprofit organizations, government, and schools to local residents. It also leveraged its municipal assessment of technology infrastructure with a regional and statewide initiative, Link Michigan. This approach brought in local partners like the Lansing Board of Water and Light, Ameritech as the telecommunications provider, and the Regional Economic Development Team.

What makes Lansing's initiative unique is that it did not just stop at understanding the supply of technology infrastructure; it also used the leveraged partnerships to gain information about how the community of Lansing was using the existing capacity of technology infrastructure and how community demand was evolving. The demand analysis indicated that there was a lack of public awareness of IT and benefits of computerization among both businesses and residents. Given the primary goal of the IT Initiative—to extend the benefits of technology to everyone in Lansing—the Infrastructure Subcommittee's first move was to look at how educational opportunities could be expanded, working with Lansing School District middle school students and a local nonprofit, the Black Child and Family Institute, to offer families the chance to connect to the Internet at home in an affordable way and to receive hardware and software training. In addition, the city worked with Lansing's Regional Chamber of Commerce to improve technology training and understanding with local businesses. Lansing's IT Initiative drove the inventory of technology infrastructure to understand how it fit into the economic development opportunities of the city's residents and businesses.

Several other cities have produced an assessment of technology infrastructure for similar economic development reasons; however, to some degree each has embedded the function of inventorying into the governing process so that the data are updated on a semi-regular basis. Roanoke's Vision 2001 2020 called for the inventory of all technology infrastructure, and the city's Department of Transportation took the necessary steps to provide various maps of fiber-optic, wireless, and other broadband infrastructure for the city. As part of the implementation of the 2001 2020 plan, the responsibility for this function remains with the Department of Transportation. But as part of the government's coordinated effort to understand the city's position in technology infrastructure and convey this to local telecommunications providers and interested parties, the plan is seen as benefiting Roanoke's economic development efforts and its transportation and planning departments as well.

Economic development concerns also drove Mesa's original assessment of technology infrastructure after it lost a desired business prospect due to its lack of connectivity. The city thought that it had adequate capacity; however, the experience made the city realize that it needed better knowledge of where technology infrastructure was located and what capacity the existing networks actually provided. In the cases of both Roanoke and Mesa, the original inventory actions were a result of intragovernmental partnerships, but after completion the information had a number of external and internal uses, serving internally as an educational device for future plans and developments and serving externally to influence private capital investment. Most importantly, both cities maintain the inventory function outside of economic development offices. The transportation, planning, and licensing related agencies are often better positioned with resources and capacity to continue updates.

Another city with an inventory of its jurisdiction's technology infrastructure is Tacoma. Tacoma sees the benefit of maintaining inventories beyond its own fiber-optic network, the Click! Network. City leaders believe that it is essential to know the location and capacity of privately provided telecommunications services in order to look to future expansion of the city's own network in underserved or newly growing areas as well as leveraging opportunities for other economic development. In general, Tacoma's municipal utility absorbs the function that the transportation and planning departments in other cities have taken with technology infrastructure inventories. Tacoma's economic development strategies regarding technology infrastructure stress the importance of coordination across departments.

Economic development may drive the initiation of technology infrastructure inventories and even one-time assessments in most of these cities, but the information gained in the process permeates multiple government agencies because of its usefulness. Where the inventory finds a home is related to which agency has the capacity and resources to continue updates while facilitating the sharing of information across multiple agencies.

Inventories for Rights-of-Way Management

The research on the technology economy suggests that cities involved in technology infrastructure are thinking about larger issues and seem to have a stake in what the future will be in their local economies regardless of their regional setting. The technology infrastructure inventories reviewed above indicate that even economic development–driven inventories served multiple local policy agendas. Although the majority of this chapter examines the relationship of infrastructure to economic development efforts at the local level, cities utilize technology infrastructure beyond this basic need. In fact, the majority of cities examined in this chapter have infrastructure inventories, whether they exist from one-shot assessments, intermittent audits, or continual update and maintenance: Roanoke has its maps for economic development and planning, San Jose its tracking of the city's level of broadband coverage; Lansing has its initiative-driven assessment for broad economic development goals, Mesa its targeted self-assessment providing needed information to a number of departments, and Tacoma its semi-private concern for the development and longevity of the Click! Network. Charlotte, North Carolina, however, stands alone among these examples in its development of its technology infrastructure inventory. Its single purpose is to allow the Department of Transportation to maintain an inventory of all private telecommunications deployments. Although economic development policymakers are aware of the inventory, the main goal of the inventory is to strictly manage the city's rights-of-way, limiting chaos and costs associated with multiple network deployments through city streets. Charlotte's single-purpose use of the inventory could be the result of its success in attracting a variety of telecommunications providers. A local economic development official reported that access, while thought to be a problem in 1998, has diminished as the city experienced large growth, with the number of fiber-optic network projects jumping from nineteen in 1999 to thirty-two in 2000.

The birth of Charlotte's technology infrastructure inventory is unique in comparison to the other cities examined in this chapter. Charlotte's impetus was not the result of a self-assessment or technology initiative. Instead, the motivation was fending off the growth of the technology economy following the passage of the Telecommunications Act of 1996 (Telecommunications Act of 1996, 1996). The act, promoted as a way to increase competition, stated that municipalities cannot prevent companies from building new networks, but they can limit where the networks are located. The extremely vague statute did not dictate what municipalities' rights were beyond that they were allowed to manage their rights-of-way in reasonable ways. According to city officials, during the boom in the late 1990s and early 2000s, Charlotte had as many as four to five companies requesting permits to deploy their networks in the same route. In response, the city decided that telecommunications providers would need to receive their permits in the same way as other utilities (sewer, water, and electricity)—they would need to apply under the same utility encroachment agreement in order for the city to track and monitor the expansions (Charlotte Department of Transportation 2005).

Charlotte placed the development of telecommunications under the management of the Department of Transportation, where other encroachment permitting processes were located. Charlotte's approach is a result of an entrepreneurial management team, from the city attorney, who had an encroachment agreement that was quickly adjusted for telecommunications issues, to several leaders in the development services and rights-of-way management sections of the transportation department. The guidelines of the interim telecommunications rights-of-way encroachment agreement provided the foundation for the city to allow the network deployments of as many as twenty-four telecommunications companies within a three-year period at the height of the technology boom. Most of these infrastructure providers were new to the city.

The city did not allow the information from this rapid expansion to disappear. Charlotte's biggest concern was that the increased development was leading to an undue burden on the city and its residents—the degradation of rights-of-way, interruption in vehicular and pedestrian traffic, damaged water lines, increased maintenance costs because the cutting of streets often results in the city having to repair 15 percent of the patches originally made by contractors, and reservation of space for future deployments. The city developed and maintained a routing map for all telecommunications infrastructure for the popular uptown area as of 1998. In addition, the city began to act as an intermediary between telecommunications providers desiring access to the same routes, suggesting that those companies lease from the main company. The resulting ventures often had telecommunications companies paying less for access to an existing network than it would cost to deploy their own network. The city's desires were met, and telecommunications companies often saved time and money. In general, Charlotte's actions have resulted in good relationships with telecommunications providers even though Charlotte is one of the more strict municipalities in its permitting requirements.

Charlotte has also been able to receive multiple benefits during the negotiation process of most encroachment agreements. Thus far, telecommunications providers have donated approximately $800,000 in conduit to the city, enabling Charlotte to connect to the state's network and deploy numerous miles of fiber-optic cable. These exchanges, as well as the strict maintenance of the rights-of-way, are done for good reason. Charlotte sits on a bed of granite that discourages making open cuts in roads for new fiber routes because the granite is too hard a substance. Most providers are only allowed to bore holes, but a limited number of these are in city streets. Instead, the majority of approved deployments are under sidewalks. Consequently, Charlotte's geographic disadvantage has resulted in a physical advantage when it comes to telecommunications network deployment, with fewer manholes in the streets.

Charlotte's role as the intermediary among telecommunications providers that are competing for market share and for space in the ground for networks has been noticed throughout the state of North Carolina. In fact, the success of the telecommunications interim encroachment agreement can to some extent be measured by the desire of surrounding cities (Greensboro, Raleigh, Winston-Salem) to replicate the agreement for their own process. Charlotte's approach is regarded as a municipal best practice. The interim encroachment agreement is still in use nine years after the passage of the Telecommunications Act. The city has started to draft a new ordinance to replace it, but the city's original agreement was sufficiently forward looking. In the event of a new ordinance, all telecommunications agreements to date will automatically convert to the new ordinance's needs and requirements.

Inventories for Licensing

The third function of inventorying technology infrastructure is also related to rights-of-way management. Instead of transportation coordination, the inventory serves as the foundation for licenses and franchises through which the city negotiates extra functionality, whether it is collected fees, joint venture opportunities, or additional infrastructure for schools, underserved areas, and/or public spaces. Mesa's E-Streets Office operates in such a manner. Mesa's inventory originated from a self-assessment of technology infrastructure described in the section above. The assessment process included multiple private and government stakeholders, such that the departments of Planning, Transportation, Public works, and Financial Services invested time and energy to make it possible. Although Mesa's desire to conduct an assessment of technology infrastructure occurred mainly due to economic development concerns, the assessment process indicated many overlapping needs among the involved departments. In order to fully utilize the information collected, the home for the inventory became the E-Streets and Licensing Broadband Development Office, but strong communication lines existed among this office and Economic Development, Transportation, and Planning.

The inventory of technology infrastructure was beneficial to the city's transportation and other planning processes encompassing the continued design and upgrade of the city's institutional network responsible for all city-related services and transportation/traffic operations. Before the assessment, the city neither had a firm understanding of where private telecommunications providers' infrastructures were located nor was it aware of the capacity of those networks. This made many of its institutional network expansions unable to leverage existing capacity without multiple evaluations and discussions with a number of carriers. At the same time, economic development efforts to recruit or accommodate business telecommunications needs required a similar chaotic process if the business did not go directly to the provider on its own. Both issues are a result of telecommunications providers' keeping information about their networks confidential. They consider any logistics regarding their networks as proprietary in order to keep their competitors in the dark.

Mesa realized that this was not an efficient situation, and that government should fulfill a basic role in telecommunications infrastructure and be an educator in the market. Mesa cobbled together the technology infrastructure information gained through the assessment in a series of maps that corresponded to the city's employment areas with fiber-optic lines, broadband services (cable modem and DSL), and wireless networks. Finding that the older employment centers had better coverage than new and developing ones, the city used this information to inform local telecommunications providers that growing areas were in need of new infrastructure. A number of providers admitted to not realizing the magnitude of this disparity, and, recognizing the strategic opportunity, some providers began to shift resources to areas with greater need. The process influenced the capital improvement plans of several telecommunications providers, but almost as important is that it opened lines of communication between the city and telecommunications providers for economic development and planning.

To institutionalize this process, the city continues to monitor telecommunications and cable deployment through the E-Streets and Licensing Broadband Development Office. The office is responsible for licensing issues for broadband telecommunications and cable communications systems as providers request use of the city's public rights-of-way. The process keeps the city aware of what type of technology infrastructure providers are deploying, and the city documents these changes. In addition, through the licensing process the city leverages the use of its rights-of-way costs in a number of ways allowable under the Telecommunications Act of 1996. For example, the city has been able to extend its network in areas where private telecommunications providers already have networks, and the negotiation process often provides the city with access or ownership at a cost less than it would incur to either purchase or build in the open market. The city also reports that some negotiations produce additional conduit or fiber-optic cable for city use, access for public uses (from cable access channels to wireless hot spots for government and schools), and service to underserved areas. Although all are important to the city, Mesa's documentation of the location and capacity of the technology infrastructure for which a license is requested is one of the most important issues for the city. It allows it to continue to monitor its technology infrastructure while supporting a number of other city goals beyond economic development.

Beyond maintaining the technology infrastructure inventory, the office through the E-Streets Initiative is responsible for a network with joint trench venture opportunities for private telecommunications providers. The office spearheads the construction of the city's new fiber-optic network deployments around the city, but mainly in the east.

Several projects and growth in the eastern part of Mesa demanded the expansion of the city's institutional network. Instead of just building the network for city purposes, the city financed and deployed additional conduits for private sale. Mesa is neither losing money nor making a profit. The city sees this added expense as a cost in facilitating broadband and infrastructure development in areas that need better services and are growing employment areas where businesses need to have access to telecommunications services. At some level, the city's financial commitment to the E-Streets Initiative is counterbalanced with the pursuit of additional city services through licensing negotiations, but each function serves to develop greater technology infrastructure and knowledge in Mesa.

The process of identifying how and why each of the highlighted cities in the analysis of inventories now has technology inventories provides a greater perspective on the use of technology infrastructure in cities. Although the nexus of technology and economic development efforts is a focus of this book, the various machinations of the technology economy in cities suggest that the boundaries of economic development with other policy actions are blurry. Technology infrastructure inventories provide a foundation for multiple strategic uses. This hints at an explanation of why the presence of an inventory had an insignificant effect on technology sector employment (see Chapter 3). Conducting and maintaining an inventory of technology infrastructure in and of itself, while an entrepreneurial enterprise, does not suggest much action toward building a local technology economy. However, the integration of multiple technology infrastructure policies, including an inventory, seems to be the more likely policy environment in these cities. How technology infrastructure is prompting a response from a variety of city departments and agencies suggests that it has strategic uses beyond the impetus driving the original collection of information.

Insights and Observations

The examination of these seven cities demonstrates a variety of methods by which local governments are seeking to shape their responses to the technology economy. Using the framework of economic development, the directions that many cities take do not necessarily conform to narrow economic development policies. Multiple types of policymakers in authority and location within government play large roles, but most of the cities' motivations to concentrate on technology infrastructure vis-à-vis the economy, technology sectors, and quality-of-life issues are a result of some recognized opportunity or challenge.

For the city of Tacoma, the need for an upgrade to the networks of their utility seemed like an appropriate time to reflect on how this investment could produce greater results for the city. Lansing's economic struggles and strong mayoral leadership refocused its approach on growth and development. Roanoke experienced a similar desire for a new economic base, and through several partnerships, designed technology infrastructure policies to create the needed environment. Mesa's loss of a desired business due to a lack of technology infrastructure surprised local policymakers enough to produce a dedicated effort and new communication models among government agencies and the private sector. In San Jose's case, the city was already in an advantaged position for looking at technology infrastructure issues, but the recession and other competing cities made the city realize that technology infrastructure investment was still needed. Charlotte's foray into technology infrastructure is limited mostly to the inventory because the private market provided enough development to meet demand, causing the city's economic development department to change its course. However, this development required diligent oversight to ensure a more structured outcome. Finally, Portland's examination of economic development opportunities suggests that the city had a lack of knowledge and concern for technology infrastructure. In honing its focus, Portland saw opportunities to create desired growth as well as provide city services needed in the Unwire Portland venture.

Vision-oriented thinking about how a city can be ready for and take advantage of the technology economy represents only one side of the technology infrastructure spectrum, which in the case of Lansing was even broader that its economic development home. However, vision by itself is not enough, as evidenced in the analysis in Chapter 3 as well as the examples presented here. Only cities that went beyond vision with multiple technology infrastructure policy actions reported greater technology economy results and successes. Integration into the economic development vision did not provide a direct enough effect, but when vision transformed into strategies, cities had success. These cities' actions demonstrate a dedication to technology economy factors and a refocusing of the way that cities are thinking about the future—whether it is economic development, transportation, or planning. In the eyes of many, technology infrastructure is no longer an isolated core infrastructure, and slowly but surely it is moving into more active uses.

As with technology infrastructure inventories, the multiple faces of technology infrastructure in these cities show its expanded influence, stimulating other planning and policy activities beyond economic development. In fact, the separation of technology infrastructure solely within economic development seems counterproductive. The blanketing effect of technology infrastructure on economic development, planning, transportation, public works, and even finance departments suggests the structural importance of this factor and is an indication that the technology economy has broad application in cities. As shown in Chapter 3, economic development strategies that address technology infrastructure are important factors to technology sector employment, yet the presence of the strategy in economic development visions or inventories alone is not sufficient. The examination of cities in this chapter indicates that this may be because both the benefits and, often, the costs are dispersed. Multiple technology infrastructure policies often have impact beyond limited targets, and as other departments become involved we see a distribution of costs across government priorities and an even greater distribution of benefits. As a true infrastructure, early planning, awareness, and coordination disperse the benefits to multiple projects and individuals, which is why many cities experienced commitment from a number of departments and agencies even if they were not sure the direct effect would be beneficial. The effects of technology have always created measurement problems, and the stories from these cities show how certain strategies or actions blur boundaries within local government and economic development, which makes it more difficult to measure the direct impact of even one strategy.

The cities examined here view technology infrastructure as an enabler of private sector development and local economic development. Whether this public-private technology infrastructure "enabling" strategy is more efficient in terms of public cost per rate of change in local job growth than the conventional firm-focused tax and expenditure subsidy has yet to be determined given the time horizon of these initiatives and the difficulty in measuring the overall effect of multiple policies. However, the commitment of local governments beyond typical economic development strategies and its influence on multiple departments and offices suggest some level of awareness that technology infrastructure is key to the future of cities' economic well-being. The research for this book suggests that we see technology infrastructure having a positive effect on a city's employment in, and beyond, the targeted technology sectors. The intersection of technology infrastructure and technology sectors is consequential to the future of local economic development, and state and local economic development policymakers may need to take notice of the comparative effectiveness of technology infrastructure in the local economic development policy sphere.

6

Local Policy Action
in the Technology Economy

A touching but erroneous American belief is that a good idea and individual know-how are all you need to change the world. But it's government not just an individual or even a company, that usually develops, backs or distributes most world-changing technology—from the Internet to the Interstate highway system.

—*Alex Marshall*

The impact of advanced telecommunications networks on global communication is more evident than the impact of these same networks upon the urban landscape, but the urban impacts of these networks may be equally profound, touching individuals more frequently (and perhaps more profoundly).

—*August E. Grant and Lon Berquist*

The impacts of the technology economy are neither concentrated nor small. A range of individuals and organizations are dealing with the implications of the technology economy in normal day-to-day operations. Application of technologies and the resulting alteration of business processes create greater efficiencies and productivity for business and individuals. The manifestation of the technology economy through cities and their policies produces yet another layer of effect on residents and businesses. The manner in which cities absorb the technology economy affects the vibrancy of local economies and municipal livability. In focusing on this tantamount intersection of local government and the forces of the technology economy, I have detailed the opportunities that the technology economy presents to cities and described how a cross-section of cities in the United States are thinking about the technology economy's role in their localities.

The Importance of Being Local

This book strives to be grounded in two worlds of technology, analyzing technology's role in the economy and in specific industries, as well as assessing the capacity and issues surrounding technology infrastructure. The interrelationship between technology sectors and technology infrastructure is consequential to future long-term growth and development. How the infrastructure supplies the innovative capacity and a supporting foundation is integral to the technology economy's effects. The intersection of these two issues creates an exciting and variable space that holds both great advantages and disadvantages for influenced geographies and ·actors. Nowhere is this intersection more variable than in local governments, with policymakers having the responsibility to prepare for the technology economy under the pressure of elections and budgets. Local governments desire opportunities that will make their cities and towns more livable, whether they provide economic benefits or quality amenities. Localities have politically viable arms with policymaking institutions and monetary powers to react to and build toward such opportunities.

Through survey and case-study analyses, I find that cities are creating direct and indirect approaches to harness the technology economy. City policy agendas demonstrate the recognition that the technology economy provides new opportunities and that cities can mold these opportunities into long-term advantages. Entrepreneurial actions do not come only from the cities already basking in technology success or those with fiscal surpluses. Nor are all cities clinging to the technology economy as an economic savior. Cities with diverse assets are able to explore and create suitable environments in which local technology economies can grow. In addition, local policies are not one-dimensional, concentrating solely on technology economy sectors and the growth generated across these sectors. Many cities recognize the link to the actual technologies that enable innovation, the technology infrastructure. City actions are examples to other cities looking for guidance, and, of perhaps even greater importance, the cumulative effect of these policies and their results indirectly shapes the technology economy of the entire nation.

City Performance in the Technology Economy

The examination of the technology economy's effect on local areas and local government activities provides a greater understanding of what types of cities are performing well in terms of technology sector employment and technology infrastructure, as well as the interrelationships between the two building blocks of the technology economy. I analyze two types of technology sectors, emphasizing the importance of human capital and innovative capacity to technology-driven growth. In focusing on firms with the highest concentrations of science and engineering human capital and innovation through research and development, my analysis of technology economy sectors unites these two factors thought to be key to the future of local economy development (Florida 2002; Eisinger 1988; Clarke and Gaile 1998; Chapple et al. 2004; Bresnahan and Gambardella 2004). The rankings of cities by technology employment in each of these sectors as well as subsectors indicate a relationship among innovation and human capital industries at the local level, with technology economy sectors showing a regional preference, or agglomeration tendencies. Where differences exist, the rankings provide insight into a city's relative advantage in human capital or innovation industries relative to other cities. The comparison of the subsectors for both technology employers and generators reveals greater variation and specialization among local economies. Thus, policymakers should seek to understand which technology sector or subsector is more likely to locate in their cities, and they should craft policies that accentuate their relative advantages while addressing their weaknesses.

Although the rankings allow for a comparison of the leading and lagging cities as well as comparison among the leaders of the subsectors, I further examine the technology economy in cities to determine what types of factors might be influencing local technology sector employment. The comparison of cities on these factors and with different levels of technology sector employment indicates where cities must focus their policy agendas—emphasizing the development of human capital and innovative capacity. I find that local telecommunications infrastructure is an important factor in explaining local technology sector employment, providing some evidence of a relationship between technology economy sectors and infrastructure investment. In particular, the multivariate regression analyses reveal that cities with large presences of technology employers, or higher average concentrations of science and engineering human capital, are also more innovative and well educated, with less of an older population. Physical telecommunications infrastructure has an impact, such that cities with greater technology employer employment have greater high-speed line density, but fewer telecommunications improvements than cities lagging in technology employer employment. Cities leading in technology generator employment, or higher-than-average concentrations of innovation, are also more innovative and well educated, and they have a larger young adult population. Local officials in these cities think about and use their telecommunications infrastructure as part of economic development strategies, but these cities have had fewer telecommunications improvements than cities lagging in technology generator employment. Overall, the analysis of ranking cities and exploring defining characteristics suggest that great disparities exist between cities performing well in the technology economy and those not performing as well. The presence of these disparities and the evidence that technology economy growth is beneficial—from higher education levels to other measures of economic prosperity—imply that there is a need for local government policy to proactively address disparities and find methods for generating leading technology environments.

City Activities in the Technology Economy

Local policymakers predominately shape their responses to the technology economy through their economic development policy agendas. Although not all cities are drawn to technology sector development, many understand that the infrastructure component of the technology economy requires attention for reasons beyond sectoral development. To examine these policy actions, I utilize the Economic Development and Technology Economy Survey to ascertain how cities are addressing the technology economy and what role technology infrastructure plays in city economic development policies. Although the survey approach method provides greater detail about local actions, two factors appear to be affecting the perspectives of city economic development officials in this survey. First, the technology economy–driven boom and bust in the late 1990s through early 2000s likely raised questions in the minds of local officials about the role of the technology economy in their own local economic arenas and might have called into question city efforts to invest in technology economy infrastructure. Second, the recession of 2001 as well as the terrorist attacks of September 11, 2001, left city officials coping with unprecedented public safety expenditures and significant economic and fiscal challenges, a marked transition from the unprecedented growth of the 1990s and early part of the new century. As a result, policymakers had little flexibility in spending on anything out-side of essential services. Nonetheless, cities face longer-term shifts from manufacturing-based, to services-based, to increasingly technology- and information-based economic growth. These economic shifts in conjunc-tion with globalization, demographic changes, and heightened tensions between state and local governments about the arrangements needed to foster economic growth create an impression that the technology economy could be too important to ignore. As local policymakers, schol-ars, and analysts contemplate the future of local economies, the opin-ions expressed by local officials, regardless of the timing of this survey, should prove helpful in identifying local issues and perceived needs.

The survey analysis reveals that cities are sensitive to the changing tides of their local economies and points to the importance that technol-ogy infrastructure plays in current and future economic stability. Yet this recognition has limited influence on local policies concerned with economic development because of three major hurdles. The first hurdle is that most local officials interested in technology infrastructure as-sessment and development are often operating in conflict with their lo-cal private infrastructure providers. Private providers often decline to increase capacity in response to government requests and even refuse to share information about the capacity of available local infrastructure because it is sensitive to competition in the local market. These public-private conflicts of interest lead to a second hurdle—a lack of infra-structure knowledge and capacity at the local level. Unlike the superior records that most cities have on core infrastructures like roads and water and utility lines, the technology infrastructure is a relative unknown in terms of location and capacity. Although some entrepreneurial cities have collected this information through permitting processes and other initiatives, those that possess this information are few in number. This fact leads to the third hurdle—that public-private conflicts and lack of information about technology infrastructure preclude the use of the in-formation as part of economic development strategies. It is difficult to identify gaps and needs without information about location and capacity.

The three hurdles underscore the disconnect between actual policies and the recognition of the technology economy's role in the future eco-nomic viability of cities. However, some local officials recognize this and are proactive in addressing these hurdles. Discovering why and how cities are able to address the technology economy through economic development policies, while addressing conflict and the lack of technology infrastructure knowledge, demonstrates the range of options available to other cities.

Local Entrepreneurial Cities in the Technology Economy

Many concerned local officials claim that it is their public duty to provide knowledge and services when there are disparities and local needs go unmet. They profess that an adequate, advanced technology infrastructure is in the public interest because it is linked to municipal quality of life, economic well-being, and the city's future vitality. In examining how seven entrepreneurial cities approach the intersection of economic development and technology infrastructure, I find that the active support of local officials and leaders is essential; however, this is often best matched with public outreach to other stakeholders in the community, especially the private market technology infrastructure providers. Cities seeking economic development gains through a better understanding and usage of technology infrastructure are active in this arena using four basic approaches. Each city is designing planning efforts and strategies with respect to the technology infrastructure and sectors in order to overcome conflict with the private sector or lack of knowledge about city technology infrastructure and competitiveness at a regional or national level. Each of these cities utilizes its technology infrastructure as an asset.

Of the four basic approaches that local governments use to integrate the technology economy into their cities' economic development and planning strategies, the first approach addresses how cities view technology infrastructure in relation to economic development efforts. A number of cities position technology infrastructure as a formal component or element of their economic development planning documents. Within the economic development plans, local policymakers view technology infrastructure as playing an instrumental role in the growth and development of business and citizenry well-being. Tacoma, Lansing, and San Jose are unique in that technology infrastructure plays a strong role in shaping the vision for economic development in their cities. As with any vision, the impetus behind this vision provides insight into the manner of their policymaking in the technology economy. In each city an opportunity presented itself, and each city recognized this opportunity and sought to institutionalize technology infrastructure as a foundation for growth.

The second approach highlights the specific policy actions cities take in terms of deploying or developing technology infrastructure as part of other economic development policy agendas. Six of the seven cities (Roanoke, Lansing, Mesa, Tacoma, San Jose, and Portland) actually offer technology infrastructure as a specific policy device or action with which the city hopes to generate growth and development. The breadth of these technology infrastructure policies is as narrow as specific infrastructure projects, like technology zones, or policies intended for specific industries, like technology businesses, but the cities also develop broader technology infrastructure policies with the hopes of generating positive returns for both business and residents, such as public wireless networks. Regardless of the breadth of the policy, cities view technology infrastructure as a key to economic development efforts.

The third approach focuses on how cities use technology infrastructure as a direct input into the cultivation of a certain type of business climate—the sectors of the technology economy. Roanoke, San Jose, Mesa, Tacoma, and Portland view technology infrastructure as an essential factor in attraction and retention of technology business. The desire to grow technology business is met by both direct and indirect investments in technology infrastructure development, from provision of capacity, like wireless networks or conduits, to creating suitable technology spaces in incubators and smart buildings. Although city policymakers target these benefits for technology businesses, the strategies often have spillover effects and influence a broader swath of business and residents. Most of the cities thinking about technology infrastructure in an entrepreneurial manner see this connection and seek to exploit it for broader benefits.

The fourth approach is a citywide or neighborhood assessment (or inventory) of technology infrastructure availability and capacity. Interestingly, city inventories are not always the direct result of an economic development policy, but inventories indicate that cities view technology infrastructure as important to the local economy and livability. Of the cities with inventories of technology infrastructure, most have found a number of strategic uses beyond the impetus for the original collection of information, and these served to gain additional support for the inventories and often expanded their influence into other planning and policy activities.

Generally, the creation and maintenance of an inventory on the location, capacity, and ownership of technology infrastructure serves three general functions. The first is related to economic development attraction, growth, and retention programs, where economic development policymakers use the information to ensure buildings or developable lands meet the functional telecommunications requirements of business prospects looking to relocate or expand in the city. The inventories of Lansing, Roanoke, Mesa, and Tacoma are a result of an economic development–driven process. Second, in some cities the Department of Transportation or Planning keeps an inventory of all private telecommunications deployments in order to strictly manage the city's rights-of-way, limiting chaos and costs associated with multiple network deployments through city streets and other facilities. Charlotte provides a good example of a transportation-oriented inventory. The third type of inventory of technology infrastructure is also related to rights-of-way management, but instead of transportation coordination, the inventory serves as the foundation for licenses and franchises through which the city negotiates for some extra functionality, whether it is collected fees, joint venture opportunities, or additional infrastructure for schools, underserved areas, and/or public spaces. Mesa's unique positioning of this management with its joint venture infrastructure deployment demonstrates this entrepreneurial approach to technology infrastructure inventories.

A consequential outcome of cities' efforts to assess and inventory their technology infrastructure is that these efforts often provide a foundation for multiple strategic uses. Spillover effects are also evident when cities integrate multiple technology infrastructure policies into citywide goals. Multiple types of policymakers in authority and location within local governments play large roles, but most of the cities' motivations to concentrate on technology infrastructure, technology sectors, and quality-of-life issues are a result of some presenting opportunity or challenge, such as the loss of business or competition for business. In the eyes of many, technology infrastructure is no longer an isolated core infrastructure, but a core infrastructure necessary for economic growth. The blanketing effect of technology infrastructure in economic development, planning, transportation, public works, and even finance departments suggests the structural importance of this factor and is an indication that the technology economy has broad application in cities.

The cities examined in Chapter 5 view technology infrastructure as an enabler of private sector development and local economic development. Whether a technology infrastructure "enabling" strategy is more efficient than traditional tax and expenditure subsidies is yet to be determined given the time horizon of these initiatives and the difficulty in measuring the overall effect of multiple technology infrastructure policies. However, the activities of local governments, beyond typical economic development strategies and across multiple departments and offices, reveal some level of citywide awareness that technology infrastructure is key to the future of cities' economic well-being. The research for this book suggests that we do indeed see technology infrastructure as having a positive effect on a city's employment level in the technology sectors. The intersection of technology infrastructure and technology sectors is consequential to the future of local economic development, and state and local economic development policymakers should take notice of the comparative effectiveness of technology infrastructure in the local economic development policy sphere.

Learning from Local Action

In utilizing a triangulation of methods—drawing on national-level data analysis, survey analysis, and case studies—I have uncovered definite patterns of technology economy activity in a variety of cities, as demonstrated in the case-study examples of Lansing, Tacoma, Roanoke, and Mesa. None of these cities has a national reputation as a thriving or existing technology center, yet each has an established policy track record in technology economy infrastructure and sectors. Viewed through a regional lens, perhaps some of these policy actions are attributable to competition with other cities in their regions that are nationally recognized technology centers or hubs. Competition from Tempe and Seattle, respectively, could create an incentive for Mesa and Tacoma to react so that their jurisdictions are more competitive and ready to gain from the spillover effects of their technology neighbors. Attempts to siphon some benefit from agglomeration economies and clustering of technology sectors does indeed seem to be a factor in some cities, but not in all local action in the technology economy.

The analysis points to three factors, in particular, that influence whether cities design economic development policies with technology infrastructure in mind. First, cities leverage existing assets and infrastructure in order to develop their technology infrastructure. In the case of Tacoma, the municipal electric utility provided the city with an opportunity to leverage public investment on a basic upgrade of the utility network to improve electrical services operation and maintenance into a telecommunications service network for city residents and business. As owner of the network, the city opted to contract with private sector telecommunications providers instead of providing the services itself. Tacoma has improved coverage throughout the city and the level of services provided. It utilizes its technology infrastructure as an asset in economic development and other planning policies, and prioritizes continued investment in and further leveraging of its assets. Mesa also leverages infrastructure to develop technology economy opportunities. Although it does not have a municipal utility, Mesa views its previous U.S. Air Force base and general aviation airport in the eastern part of the city as a target employment area and recognizes that it could not be successful without the support of technology infrastructure. The construction of the East Loop and E-Streets joint venture in this location demonstrates how attention to technology economy needs provides the impetus to leverage existing physical infrastructures, whether they be a local utility or available and usable parcels of land.

How cities attend to integrating technology infrastructure into existing planning structures and policies is predicated on an understanding of what enables cities to recognize opportunities. The comments of public officials and results from the cases indicate that leadership is essential to this process. A number of stakeholders are key, but each frames technology infrastructure as a tool beyond something that the private sector can provide. The best example from the presented cases is the leadership of the mayor in Lansing. Nevertheless, in all cities, the support of city officials and department leaders is necessary for the creation and maintenance of technology infrastructure policies. Mesa's economic development strategy extends across several governmental agencies because of the leadership throughout economic development, E-Streets, transportation, and public works. San Jose's current study of whether the city should extend the public-supported wireless network is a follow-on to the mayor's priority for 100 percent broadband access in the city. Leadership is consequential to city development of a technology infrastructure focus for economic development and other uses.

Another key factor that seems to be prevalent in cities looking to technology infrastructure as part of their future policies and strategies is investment in the assessment and mapping of their technology infrastructure. Inventories serve as a starting place for cities exploring how to be ready for and take advantage of technology economy development. As the foundation for a number of technology economy strategies, technology infrastructure assessments seem to be a necessary component in developing a holistic policy agenda in the technology economy. Understanding where technology infrastructure is in terms of location and capacity enables cities to more clearly address strengths and weaknesses. Some cities opt to publicly invest in infrastructure, from wireless networks to complete fiber-optic networks. Others use the information gleaned to educate multiple private sector providers about areas that lack service and where opportunities exist; this approach encourages future private investment to address these underserved areas. Once the assessments are completed, some cities continue to maintain records of technology infrastructure improvements from both public and private sector deployments. In addition to the leveraging of existing assets and leadership, the knowledge of technology infrastructure is a foundation for most policy maneuvering as cities seek to design and influence their futures in the technology economy.

Efforts of cities to design technology economy policies utilize a number of common methods. Two components are instrumental to the design process and the desired outcomes. Although a particular problem might kick-start a city on the path of technology economy development, most cities move forward relying on the input of multiple local stakeholders. The process of defining the vision for city efforts and how the technology economy and infrastructure correspond with local needs and desires is a necessary step for broad changes. Leveraging of existing assets, leadership, and technology infrastructure assessments are essential to establishing the justification for local endeavors. Cities designing an overall technology economy approach necessarily prioritize working with the community and the private sector. Focusing on the future of a city's economy and quality of life, the creation of targets and policies that deliver community benefits cannot be a second-tier consideration. As with the IT initiative in Lansing and the public wireless study in San Jose, cities incorporate the benefits and costs into all segments of the community as part of the vision and design process. This focus also suggests that cities build relationships with the private sector in order to understand how the technology economy is affecting existing and targeted businesses. Assessing the needs of the community and the private sector provides a more complete vision of primary goals and objectives of technology economy policies. Lansing, Mesa, Portland, Roanoke, San Jose, and Tacoma engage the private sector in their economic development and planning processes. Private telecommunications providers can also be part of this dialogue; the processes in Mesa, Lansing, San Jose, and Portland stress how collaboration between local governments and private telecommunications providers can create positive results and relationships for future policy development. Cities that create a role for the community and the private sector design technology economy–focused solutions that have multiple spillovers.

The analysis of local governments in the technology economy from national and survey data comparison and case studies suggests a model of local government action. I find that a series of factors points to why and how cities utilize economic development policy and the building blocks of the technology economy. The case studies demonstrate what cities are doing at the ground level, which would be overlooked with other methods. What I glean from these cities, combined with the data results, suggests a course of action for cities wanting to harness technology economy growth. A variety of cities have options, and in focusing on assets that can be leveraged, building supportive leadership, prioritizing exploratory assessments of technology infrastructure, and enlisting the participation of community and private sector actors, cities are better positioned to examine how local strategies can address technology economy changes and create local opportunities.

Technology Economy Policy in the
Intergovernmental Arena

Cities are active in the technology arena, and my research highlights both city activities and barriers to these activities. Evidence of disparities among cities in the technology economy indicates that cities can and should be proactive in shaping their local technology economy. However, some cities report that they lack economic development strategies to address the technology economy because of a lack of technology infrastructure knowledge and the existence of public-private conflict over this asset. The case studies demonstrate how some cities are traversing these hurdles, stressing the importance of communication, planning for multiple solutions, and using knowledge accumulated to steer relations with the private sector. Entrepreneurial actions of local governments imply that public investment in the technology economy is less about physical infrastructure in which the private sector has a comparative advantage, and more about the information and knowledge cities create in the course of developing effective communication lines, within government and between government and the private sector. For cities to be successful in their public investment in the technology economy, local governments must have the power to explore alternatives and craft policies to target technology economy growth.

All of the conclusions of this research point to the need for a strong local role within a system that enables local policy action and activities to shape a technology economy response. The powers of local governments, however, are often constrained in the intergovernmental arena. By the nature of their design, cities are creatures of the states in which they are located. As corporations of their state government, states control and monitor the powers of cities through their articles of incorporation as well as various legislative actions through time. Cities may not be as nimble in technology infrastructure because of these structural intergovernmental relationships. Furthermore, technology and telecommunications policy is an arena that is often controlled by state and federal governments. Although the need for a strong local government role is apparent from the analysis of cities in technology economy, current policies of states and federal governments determine what roles cities can play and limit possibilities. Local governments, thus, are often reactive to these regulations. The constraints placed on localities from recent actions and policies at the federal and state levels of government hinder some cities' ability to take advantage of opportunities that technology infrastructure offers. At other times, a lack of policy and regulation creates a void in a space from which localities could otherwise benefit.

Federal Decisions Shaping Local Actions

Federal decisions and nondecisions affect local authority in technology infrastructure policy. Perhaps the most familiar federal policy action is the Telecommunications Act of 1996. The first massive overhaul of communications law since 1934, the Telecommunications Act addressed the growing telecommunications arena and was intended to create greater competition among telecommunications providers and lead to extra deployment of advanced telecommunications infrastructures and services during a period of time in which this industry was already booming. However, the story of the Telecommunications Act is one of unrealized expectations. Policymakers could not have foreseen the recession, the fervor of mergers between large telecommunications providers—from Verizon's emerging out of GTE and Bell Atlantic to the recent Sprint and Nextel merger—and the negative effect these developments would have on broadband deployment. The growth of broadband services has not even kept pace with other countries. During the 2004 election cycle, President George W. Bush made a call for greater broadband deployment that would be both universal and affordable by 2007. But the Bush administration has not provided a vision or any type of efforts to deliver on this call (Bleha 2005). In fact, from 2001 to 2003 the United States fell from fourth to thirteenth in global broadband Internet penetration, according to International Telecommunication Union (ITU) annual reports (International Telecommunication Union 2003; Bleha 2005). To make matters worse, the ITU's latest annual report of 2005 shows another decline to sixteenth place, with the United States now lagging behind South Korea, Hong Kong, Canada, and Japan, to name a just few (International Telecommunication Union 2005b).

The federal government's willingness to leave broadband development in the hands of the private sector has not produced great results. City leaders are looking at the lack of services a decade after the Telecommunications Act and wondering how to fill significant gaps in services and availability of broadband. From a local government perspective, the Telecommunications Act protected the powers of local governments so that they could manage their rights-of-way (Telecommunications Act of 1996, 1996). This has aided some cities, like Charlotte, in their efforts to control the chaos of the late 1990s and early 2000s growth, but overall, most cities lack authority to influence a process that could result in better services in their jurisdictions. Cities are left on their own to deal with local telecommunications providers. In addition, the Federal Communications Commission ruled that cable modem broadband services are information services and not telecommunications services. The Supreme Court upheld the ruling, which decreased local governments' abilities to collect franchise fees from this growing segment of the market. Such federal government preemption of local authority to levy telecommunications taxes and fees and localities involvement in providing telecommunications services is part of an ongoing, high-conflict policy debate, as evidenced by two pieces of proposed legislation before the U.S. Congress. Representative Pete Sessions' Preserving Innovation in Telecom Act of 2005 (H.R. 2726) and Senator John Ensign's Broadband Investment and Consumer Choice Act (S. 1504) purport to encourage widespread investment, innovation, and competition for telecommunications services in U.S. cities, mimicking the language of the 1996 Act

(U.S. Congress, Senate 2005a; U.S. Congress, House of Representatives 2005). However, both pieces of legislation propose that the only way this can occur is if the public sector discontinues any provision or attempt to provide telecommunications services on their own, in essence, by not competing. In prohibiting municipal governments from offering telecommunications, information, or cable services, telecommunications providers will have less competition and be able to invest with less risk.

Local governments see this movement as further restriction of their ability to tap a new form of economic growth, even though many cities would never take on the investment of building and providing telecommunications services or leasing their infrastructure. In an attempt to prevent the loss of local authority, local governments have their own legislation, introduced by Senators Frank R. Lautenberg and John McCain in the Community Broadband Act of 2005 (S. 1294) (U.S. Congress, Senate 2005b). The proposed legislation ensures that states cannot prevent municipalities from offering high-speed Internet access to citizens if the local municipalities wish to do so, but municipalities cannot forgo state, federal, or municipal telecommunications laws or create anti-competitive situations in favor of other activities with municipal laws. The interaction of federal and state legislative authorities on these issues is of a great concern to local government stakeholders. The perception that state and federal initiatives are under the powers of the private market telecommunications providers and their substantial lobby increases the amount of tension and local public-private sector conflict when cities are examining methods of engaging in the technology economy.

State Decisions Shaping Local Actions

Local officials describe the process of creating advanced technology infrastructures across a community, regardless of income, race, or type of business, as a public service because unlike federal laws governing telephone service, no laws ensure universal service of broadband or any other infrastructure capacity. The result is many gaps in service and underserved areas. A recent U.S. Supreme Court ruling concerning the cities in Missouri proved to be a setback for these "activist cities" (*Nixon v. Missouri Municipal League* 2004). Local authorities in Missouri sought to become telecommunications providers in their cities, but the state's attorney general took the position that the Telecommunications Act of 1996 did not overrule the state's law forbidding cities in Missouri to offer those services. The Supreme Court agreed. Although a number of states already had laws explicitly forbidding a locality to enter into the telecommunications business, since the Supreme Court ruling, the private telecommunications industry has used the Missouri decision to lobby numerous state legislatures for laws that forbid or limit a municipality's ability to build and finance telecommunications infrastructure networks and/or offer services. In 2005, fourteen states have proposed such municipal barriers and five enacted them, while fourteen states enacted municipal barriers before 2005 (Baller 2005; American Public Power Association 2004).

Some of the proposed and enacted laws prevent localities from engaging in infrastructure development; however, most are placing a number of roadblocks in a locality's way. For example, local private providers must be given the right of first refusal in providing better infrastructure to the city before a city can plan a local option. States are requiring that cities gain approval for projects through local referenda or mandate that projects be financed with general obligation bonds, instead of revenue bonds that would be paid off from the infrastructure projects' revenues. State laws also restrict cities' abilities to lease or sell built infrastructure capacity and services at rates below private sector rates. All of these state laws serve to keep cities out of a very important policy arena. Federal Trade Commissioner Jon Leibowitz sums up the problem:

> Underlying the incumbents' position is the view that regulation—in this case, in the form of state prohibitions or restrictions on municipal broadband—is necessary to protect the market. It is a somewhat surprising argument coming from the phone and cable companies. Usually with both hands on the throttle they straightforwardly argue for deregulation— and usually I support them. But here they are using sleight-of-hand: seeking deregulation for themselves yet asking states to raise barriers to competition for others. We should stick with their general position that it's better to compete than regulate. And we should apply that principle here. (Leibowitz 2005, 5)

Similar to the interaction between traditional infrastructure and economic development, cities in the technology economy need to have some ability to influence and control the development of infrastructure that is associated with new sources of economic growth.

Beyond state legislation serving as a municipal barrier to deploying technology infrastructure, the private telecommunications lobby is seeking to transfer local franchise rights and fee collections to the states in the attempt to arrive at one uniform agreement governing all jurisdictions. These actions are a quick way for regional phone companies to enter local video markets to compete against cable and satellite companies without having to negotiate a franchise agreement with individual municipalities (Vaida 2005). Although cable satellite companies want their new video competitors to be subject to the same local regulatory process, these policies are also likely to have substantial consequences for local government autonomy. Depending on how much local governments rely on telecommunications taxes and fees, and how a state's collection of these would be redistributed, local finances could be drastically affected. Although some legislation would establish some percentage as a franchise fee for localities to collect, little is known about whether local government levying of taxes and fees is a burden on the telecommunications industry, above and beyond other forms of business taxation and fee activity. Such actions in state legislatures without a better understanding of this situation could be detrimental to local governments, stripping them of powers to treat different pieces of telecommunications in similar ways. It may be too late in the state of Texas. Governor Rick Perry recently signed a bill that allows regional phone companies to apply for a single statewide franchise; however, the cable industry in Texas filed a suit to block the legislation (Vaida 2005).

A Role for Local Governments

The conclusions of this research directly contradict much of the action at the state and federal government levels. As the lessons from the analysis indicate, the disparities that exist in the technology economy and the benefits that cities can gain with more structured and focused participation in technology economy policy, including technology infrastructure, point to the need for a strong local role. However, state and federal actions, often at the promotion of private telecommunications industry, are pushing to limit the flexibility of local governments and their decision making in the technology infrastructure space of the technology economy. Much of the legislative actions posing municipal barriers to entry and loss of local authority in the telecommunications arena limit the options of cities on the wrong side of a spatial digital divide. However, these activities also affect cities that just want to have more capacity and access and look to private and public sector relationships that could provide such opportunities.

Proponents of federal and state legislation frame the argument as if municipal action is the main barrier to private telecommunications competition and expansion. Yet, a decade since the Telecommunications Act, the private telecommunications landscape looks very different than what many expected, with significant gaps in service remaining despite a decade of private control. Proponents of municipal barriers claim that local governments are in the way of progress and are imposing greater costs on private providers, which in turn limits their return on investment. The numbers of localities jumping into the telecommunications services game are small enough that it is hard to believe that actions of a few are really the cause of less-than-expected private telecommunications expansion. In addition, most of the municipal actors are located in areas that the private providers have overlooked time and time again, most often due to a perceived lack of demand in those areas. However, if the case studies of cities in this research are any indication, a very different story emerges in regard to private and public roles. Most of the entrepreneurial cities aim for a close collaboration between local governments and the private providers. In the cases where the public and private sectors worked together and shared information, there is evidence of both private and public community benefits. A disconnect exists between what is occurring in these cities and the prevalent federal and state lobbying messages. Most local governments view their role as steering the boat and promoting better investment decisions in the private market through information exchange. They recognize the importance of technology infrastructure investment in their local economies, but they do not want to be redlined out of traditional private market expansions or have the authority to address the lack of capacity on their own.

The examination of the technology economy at the local level provides a number of key insights into what the mechanisms at work are as well as the local actions that are proactively addressing how the technology economy can provide opportunity and advantages. Identification of the hurdles as well as the many methods that exist to assist in the traversing of those hurdles points to the need for better policymaking at all levels of government. Policymakers should recognize the consequences of the technology economy on cities and the importance of local government actions in preparing for these changes. Cities that develop institutions that support and guide technology economy policy serve as guides to cities just beginning to recognize a need to respond. They create learning opportunities, for example, in fostering collaboration across multiple governmental agencies and the private sector. Other levels of government can also facilitate improved local policy. For example, in the state of Oregon, the legislature created the Oregon Telecommunications Coordinating Council (ORTCC) to "study alternative approaches to providing coordinated statewide, regional and local telecommunication services, including providing services to unserved or underserved areas of the state," and to "study the manner in which telecommunication investments can be coordinated to facilitate partnerships between the public sector and the private sector and between state and local governments" (Oregon Telecommunications Coordinating Council 2001). The facilitation of these actions at the state and local level in collaboration with the private sector demonstrates a holistic approach that is in agreement with the conclusions emerging from this research. How and when cities address the technology economy affect their future economic vitality. If localities have the authority to react with the support of state and federal governments, local policymaking will be prepared for an era of considerable public investment in the technology economy.

Appendices

Appendix A

NAICS Codes for Technology Employers and Technology Generators

Technology employers	Technology generators	NAICS codes 1997–2001	NAICS codes 2002	Industry name
X		211100	211100	Oil and gas extraction
X		211111	211111	Crude petroleum and natural gas extraction
X	X	325100	325100	Basic chemical manufacturing
X	X	325110	325110	Petrochemical manufacturing
X	X	325120	325120	Industrial gas manufacturing
X	X	325131	325131	Inorganic dye and pigment manufacturing
X	X	325182	325182	Carbon black manufacturing
X	X	325188	325188	All other basic inorganic chemical manufacturing
X	X	325192	325192	Cyclic crude and intermediate manufacturing
X	X	325199	325199	All other basic organic chemical manufacturing
X	X	325211	325211	Plastics material and resin manufacturing
	X	325212	325212	Synthetic rubber manufacturing
		325400	325400	Pharmaceutical and medicine manufacturing
X		325411	325411	Medicinal and botanical manufacturing
X		325412	325412	Pharmaceutical preparation manufacturing
X		325413	325413	In-vitro diagnostic substance manufacturing
X		325414	325414	Biological product (except diagnostic) manufacturing
X		333200	333200	Industrial machinery manufacturing
X		333210	333210	Sawmill and woodworking machinery manufacturing
X		333220	333220	Plastics and rubber industry machinery manufacturing
X		333292	333292	Textile machinery manufacturing
X		333293	333293	Printing machinery and equipment manufacturing

		Code	Description
X		333294	Food product machinery manufacturing
X		333295	Semiconductor machinery manufacturing
X		333298	All other industrial machinery manufacturing
X		333300	Commercial and service industry machinery manufacturing
X		333313	Office machinery manufacturing
X		333314	Optical instrument and lens manufacturing
X		333315	Photographic and photocopying equipment manufacturing
X		333319	Other commercial and service industry machinery manufacturing
X	X	334100	Computer and peripheral equipment manufacturing
X	X	334111	Electronic computer manufacturing
X	X	334113	Computer terminal manufacturing
X	X	334119	Other computer peripheral equipment manufacturing
X	X	334200	Communications equipment manufacturing
X	X	334210	Telephone apparatus manufacturing
X	X	334220	Radio and television broadcasting and wireless communications equipment manufacturing
X	X	334290	Other communications equipment manufacturing
X		334300	Audio and video equipment manufacturing
X		334310	Audio and video equipment manufacturing
X	X	334400	Semiconductor and other electronic component manufacturing
X	X	334412	Bare printed circuit board manufacturing
X	X	334413	Semiconductor and related device manufacturing
X	X	334414	Electronic capacitor manufacturing
X	X	334415	Electronic resistor manufacturing
X	X	334417	Electronic connector manufacturing
X	X	334418	Printed circuit assembly (electronic assembly) manufacturing
X	X	334419	Other electronic component manufacturing
X	X	334500	Navigational, measuring, electromedical, and control instruments manufacturing

Appendix A *(continued)*

Technology employers	Technology generators	NAICS codes 1997–2001	NAICS codes 2002	Industry name
X	X	334510	334510	Electromedical and electrotherapeutic apparatus manufacturing
X	X	334511	334511	Search, detection, navigation, guidance, aeronautical, and nautical system and instrument manufacturing
X	X	334512	334512	Automatic environmental control manufacturing for residential, commercial, and appliance use
X	X	334513	334513	Instruments and related products manufacturing for measuring, displaying, and controlling industrial process variables
X	X	334514	334514	Totalizing fluid meter and counting device manufacturing
X	X	334515	334515	Instrument manufacturing for measuring and testing electricity and electrical signals
X	X	334516	334516	Analytical laboratory instrument manufacturing
X	X	334517	334517	Irradiation apparatus manufacturing
X	X	334519	334519	Other measuring and controlling device manufacturing
X		336400	336400	Aerospace product and parts manufacturing
X		336411	336411	Aircraft manufacturing
X		336412	336412	Aircraft engine and engine parts manufacturing
X		336413	336413	Other aircraft parts and auxiliary equipment manufacturing
X		336419	336419	Other guided missile and space vehicle parts and auxiliary equipment manufacturing
X		421400	423410	Professional and commercial equipment and supplies merchant wholesalers
X		421410	423410	Photographic equipment and supplies merchant wholesalers
X	X	511200	511200	Software publishers
X	X	511210	511210	Software publishers

X		513390	517900	Other telecommunications
X		514191	518100	Internet service providers and web search portals
X		514191	518111	Internet service providers
X		514199	516100	Internet publishing and broadcasting
X		514199	516110	Internet publishing and broadcasting (pt.)
X		514210	518200	Data processing, hosting, and related services
X	X	541300	541300	Architectural, engineering, and related services
X	X	541310	541310	Architectural services
X	X	541330	541330	Engineering services
X	X	541370	541370	Surveying and mapping (except geophysical) services
X	X	541380	541380	Testing laboratories
X	X	541500	541500	Computer systems design and related services
X	X	541511	541511	Custom computer programming services
X	X	541512	541512	Computer systems design services
X	X	541600	541600	Management, scientific, and technical consulting services
X		541611	541611	Administrative management and general management consulting services
X		541612	541612	Human resources and executive search consulting services
X		541613	541613	Marketing consulting services
X		541614	541614	Process, physical distribution, and logistics consulting services
X		541618	541618	Other management consulting services
X		541620	541620	Environmental consulting services
X		541690	541690	Other scientific and technical consulting services
X	X	541700	541700	Scientific research and development services
X	X	541710	541710	Research and development in the physical, engineering, and life sciences
X	X	541720	541720	Research and development in the social sciences and humanities

Note: X denotes that the industry is included in the sector for that column heading; pt. denotes subset of the industry.

Appendix B

NAICS Codes for Technology Employers and Technology Generators Subsectors

Technology Employers: C: chemicals, petrochemicals, and pharmaceuticals; D: defense-related; H: hardware and communications equipment; M: manufacturing machinery and instruments; S: services research and development; SW: software and Internet services

Technology Generators: C: chemicals and petrochemicals; H: hardware and communications equipment; M: manufacturing instruments; S: services research and development; SW: software

Technology employers	Technology generators	NAICS codes 1997–2001	NAICS codes 2002	Industry name
C		211100	211100	Oil and gas extraction
C		211111	211111	Crude petroleum and natural gas extraction
C	C	325100	325100	Basic chemical manufacturing
C	C	325110	325110	Petrochemical manufacturing
C	C	325120	325120	Industrial gas manufacturing
C	C	325131	325131	Inorganic dye and pigment manufacturing
C	C	325182	325182	Carbon black manufacturing
C	C	325188	325188	All other basic inorganic chemical manufacturing
C	C	325192	325192	Cyclic crude and intermediate manufacturing
C	C	325199	325199	All other basic organic chemical manufacturing
C	C	325211	325211	Plastics material and resin manufacturing
C	C	325212	325212	Synthetic rubber manufacturing
	C	325400	325400	Pharmaceutical and medicine manufacturing
C		325411	325411	Medicinal and botanical manufacturing
C		325412	325412	Pharmaceutical preparation manufacturing
C		325413	325413	In-vitro diagnostic substance manufacturing

	Code		Description
C	325414	325414	Biological product (except diagnostic) manufacturing
M	333200	333200	Industrial machinery manufacturing
M	333210	333210	Sawmill and woodworking machinery manufacturing
M	333220	333220	Plastics and rubber industry machinery manufacturing
M	333292	333292	Textile machinery manufacturing
M	333293	333293	Printing machinery and equipment manufacturing
M	333294	333294	Food product machinery manufacturing
M	333295	333295	Semiconductor machinery manufacturing
M	333298	333298	All other industrial machinery manufacturing
M	333300	333300	Commercial and service industry machinery manufacturing
M	333313	333313	Office machinery manufacturing
M	333314	333314	Optical instrument and lens manufacturing
M	333315	333315	Photographic and photocopying equipment manufacturing
M	333319	333319	Other commercial and service industry machinery manufacturing
H	334100	334100	Computer and peripheral equipment manufacturing
H	334111	334111	Electronic computer manufacturing
H	334113	334113	Computer terminal manufacturing
H	334119	334119	Other computer peripheral equipment manufacturing
H	334200	334200	Communications equipment manufacturing
H	334210	334210	Telephone apparatus manufacturing
H	334220	334220	Radio and television broadcasting and wireless communications equipment manufacturing
H	334290	334290	Other communications equipment manufacturing
H	334300	334300	Audio and video equipment manufacturing
H	334310	334310	Audio and video equipment manufacturing
H	334400	334400	Semiconductor and other electronic component manufacturing
H	334412	334412	Bare printed circuit board manufacturing
H	334413	334413	Semiconductor and related device manufacturing
H	334414	334414	Electronic capacitor manufacturing
H	334415	334415	Electronic resistor manufacturing

Appendix B *(continued)*

Technology employers	Technology generators	NAICS codes 1997–2001	NAICS codes 2002	Industry name
H	H	334417	334417	Electronic connector manufacturing
H	H	334418	334418	Printed circuit assembly (electronic assembly) manufacturing
H	H	334419	334419	Other electronic component manufacturing
M	M	334500	334500	Navigational, measuring, electromedical, and control instruments manufacturing
M	M	334510	334510	Electromedical and electrotherapeutic apparatus manufacturing
M	M	334511	334511	Search, detection, navigation, guidance, aeronautical, and nautical system and instrument manufacturing
M	M	334512	334512	Automatic environmental control manufacturing for residential, commercial, and appliance use
M	M	334513	334513	Instruments and related products manufacturing for measuring, displaying, and controlling industrial process variables
M	M	334514	334514	Totalizing fluid meter and counting device manufacturing
M	M	334515	334515	Instrument manufacturing for measuring and testing electricity and electrical signals
M	M	334516	334516	Analytical laboratory instrument manufacturing
M	M	334517	334517	Irradiation apparatus manufacturing
M	M	334519	334519	Other measuring and controlling device manufacturing
D		336400	336400	Aerospace product and parts manufacturing
D		336411	336411	Aircraft manufacturing
D		336412	336412	Aircraft engine and engine parts manufacturing
D		336413	336413	Other aircraft parts and auxiliary equipment manufacturing
D		336419	336419	Other guided missile and space vehicle parts and auxiliary equipment manufacturing
S		421400	423410	Professional and commercial equipment and supplies merchant wholesalers
S		421410	423410	Photographic equipment and supplies merchant wholesalers

SW	S	NAICS	NAICS	
SW		511200	511200	Software publishers
SW		511210	511210	Software publishers
SW		513390	517900	Other telecommunications
SW		513390	517910	Other telecommunications
SW		514191	518100	Internet service providers and web search portals
SW		514191	518111	Internet service providers
SW		514199	516100	Internet publishing and broadcasting
SW		514199	516110	Internet publishing and broadcasting (pt.)
SW		514210	518200	Data processing, hosting, and related services
SW		514210	518210	Data processing, hosting, and related services
S	S	541300	541300	Architectural, engineering, and related services
S	S	541310	541310	Architectural services
S	S	541330	541330	Engineering services
S	S	541370	541370	Surveying and mapping (except geophysical) services
S	S	541380	541380	Testing laboratories
S	S	541500	541500	Computer systems design and related services
S	S	541511	541511	Custom computer programming services
S	S	541512	541512	Computer systems design services
S	S	541600	541600	Management, scientific, and technical consulting services
S		541611	541611	Administrative management and general management consulting services
S		541612	541612	Human resources and executive search consulting services
S		541613	541613	Marketing consulting services
S		541614	541614	Process, physical distribution, and logistics consulting services
S		541618	541618	Other management consulting services
S		541620	541620	Environmental consulting services
S		541690	541690	Other scientific and technical consulting services
S	S	541700	541700	Scientific research and development services
S	S	541710	541710	Research and development in the physical, engineering, and life sciences
S	S	541720	541720	Research and development in the social sciences and humanities

Note: X denotes that the industry is included in the sector for that column heading; pt. denotes subset of the industry.

Appendix C

Descriptive Statistics, City Characteristics, and Technology Employment

	Number of cities	Minimum	Maximum	Mean/ Mode	Standard deviation
% Technology employer employment	252	.19	36.64	4.17	3.50
% Technology generator employment	252	.00	32.61	2.82	2.97
Employment growth rate	252	−12.95	140.47	7.55	16.04
Patents per 1,000 population	252	.04	34.28	3.13	4.07
Unemployment rate	224	.10	18.20	4.739	2.2965
Per capita income	182	10,000	50,000	24,070	7,766
Median household income	252	24,221	90,859	43,600.57	15,669.47
% Poverty	252	1.36	32.30	12.13	6.99
Housing affordability rate	252	.12	.96	.4616	.13953
Population 2000	252	10,232	8,008,278	62,830.48	283,627.81
% College graduates	252	1.96	37.74	16.28	7.40
% Black	252	.14	81.81	9.87	14.55
% Age 25–34	252	4.90	16.76	10.55	2.12
% Over age 64	252	2.81	35.15	13.31	5.26
% Violent crime	104	1.63	28.71	9.95	5.31
Urban area/cluster	252	0	1	UA	N/A
Principal city	252	0	1	NPC	N/A

	N	Min	Max	Mean	SD
Metropolitan/micropolitan	252	0	1	Metro	N/A
Region	252	0	3	Midwest	N/A
Metropolitan bandwidth per pop.	252	.00	3.15	.11	.331
High-speed lines per 1,000 pop.	252	.00	.74	.17	.16
High-speed lines per square mile	252	.01	12.00	1.12	1.64
Wireless towers per 1,000 pop.	188	.02	.66	.09	.09
Wireless towers per square mile	116	0	3.01	.22	.27
Fiber available	252	0	1	Yes	N/A
Telecom improvements	238	0	1	Yes	N/A
Telecom inventory	243	0	1	No	N/A
Telecom ED plan	247	0	1	No	N/A
Telecom strategy usage	238	0	1	Yes	N/A

Sources: Technology sector and total employment (U.S. Census Bureau 2001b), patents (Hall, Jaffe, and Trajtenberg 2001), unemployment, incomes, poverty, and housing affordability rate (ratio of median family income to median value of owner-occupied housing), population, college graduates, race, and age categories (U.S. Census Bureau 2000a), crime (U.S. Federal Bureau of Investigation 1999), UA = urban area and UC = urban cluster (U.S. Census Bureau 2000c), NPC = not a principal city of the metropolitan or micropolitan statistical area (U.S. Census Bureau 2004), regions (U.S. Census Bureau 2002b), metropolitan bandwidth (Gorman 2004), high-speed lines (Federal Communications Commission 2002), wireless towers (SpectraSite 2004), remaining variables from survey (Hackler 2002).

Appendix D

List of 252 Cities Responding to Economic Development and Technology Economy Survey

Hoover	AL	Tallahassee	FL	Grand Island	NE
Ozark	AL	Tamarac	FL	Concord	NH
Prattville	AL	Albany	GA	Manchester	NH
Tuscaloosa	AL	Atlanta	GA	Brick	NJ
Little Rock	AR	College Park	GA	Old Bridge	NJ
North Little Rock	AR	Roswell	GA	Passaic	NJ
Casa Grande	AZ	Hilo	HI	Plainfield	NJ
Flagstaff	AZ	Council Bluffs	IA	Vineland	NJ
Mesa	AZ	Alton	IL	Albuquerque	NM
Prescott	AZ	Centralia	IL	Roswell	NM
Alameda	CA	Champaign	IL	Las Vegas	NV
Bakersfield	CA	Chicago	IL	North Las Vegas	NV
Buena Park	CA	Chicago Heights	IL	Reno	NV
Burbank	CA	Collinsville	IL	Sparks	NV
Camarillo	CA	Evanston	IL	Hempstead	NY
Carson	CA	Franklin Park	IL	New York City	NY
Chino	CA	Glenview	IL	Niagara Falls	NY
Clovis	CA	Joliet	IL	Schenectady	NY
Concord	CA	Kankakee	IL	Brunswick	OH
Costa Mesa	CA	Lombard	IL	Chillicothe	OH
Cudahy	CA	Moline	IL	Gahanna	OH
Downey	CA	Palatine	IL	Garfield Heights	OH
Encinitas	CA	Schaumburg	IL	Huber Heights	OH
Escondido	CA	Urbana	IL	Maple Heights	OH
Fairfield	CA	Waukegan	IL	Solon	OH
Garden Grove	CA	Westmont	IL	Springboro	OH
Glendale	CA	Elkhart	IN	Toledo	OH
Hanford	CA	Lebanon	IN	Westlake	OH
La Palma	CA	Logansport	IN	Wickliffe	OH
Lodi	CA	South Bend	IN	Broken Arrow	OK
Loma Linda	CA	Atchison	KS	Oklahoma City	OK
Long Beach	CA	Dodge City	KS	Shawnee	OK
Los Alamitos	CA	Parsons	KS	Stillwater	OK
Los Angeles	CA	Pittsburg	KS	Grants Pass	OR
Merced	CA	Wichita	KS	La Grande	OR
Monrovia	CA	Frankfort	KY	Portland	OR
Montebello	CA	Louisville	KY	The Dalles	OR
Monterey Park	CA	Madisonville	KY	Abington	PA
Morgan Hill	CA	Baton Rouge	LA	Hazleton	PA
Oakland	CA	Jennings	LA	Smithfield	RI
Palm Springs	CA	Monroe	LA	Woonsocket	RI
Pasadena	CA	New Orleans	LA	Greenville	SC

Pleasanton	CA	Boston	MA	Sioux Falls	SD
Rancho Cucamonga	CA	Lowell	MA	Watertown	SD
Rialto	CA	Mansfield	MA	Athens	TN
Ridgecrest	CA	Northampton	MA	Bryan	TX
Sacramento	CA	Westwood	MA	Corpus Christi	TX
San Carlos	CA	Weymouth	MA	Dallas	TX
San Diego	CA	Baltimore	MD	El Paso	TX
San Jose	CA	Bowie	MD	Harlingen	TX
San Leandro	CA	Augusta	ME	Keller	TX
San Mateo	CA	Bangor	ME	Kerrville	TX
Santa Ana	CA	Ann Arbor	MI	Lancaster	TX
Santa Cruz	CA	Dearborn	MI	Longview	TX
Santa Monica	CA	Dearborn Heights	MI	Marshall	TX
Sunnyvale	CA	Lansing	MI	Mission	TX
Union City	CA	Lincoln Park	MI	Orange	TX
Vacaville	CA	Muskegon	MI	Port Arthur	TX
West Covina	CA	Taylor	MI	Round Rock	TX
Whittier	CA	Troy	MI	San Marcos	TX
Colorado Springs	CO	Walker	MI	The Colony	TX
Fort Collins	CO	Westland	MI	Weatherford	TX
Lakewood	CO	Cottage Grove	MN	Ogden	UT
Bristol	CT	Lakeville	MN	Salt Lake City	UT
Hamden	CT	Minnetonka	MN	Sandy	UT
Ledyard	CT	Moorhead	MN	South Salt Lake	UT
Manchester	CT	St. Cloud	MN	West Jordan	UT
Simsbury	CT	St. Louis Park	MN	West Valley	UT
West Haven	CT	Winona	MN	Hampton	VA
Cocoa Beach	FL	Worthington	MN	Lynchburg	VA
Coral Springs	FL	Columbia	MO	Newport News	VA
Davie	FL	Farmington	MO	Roanoke	VA
De Land	FL	Gladstone	MO	Salem	VA
Delray Beach	FL	Kansas City	MO	Bellevue	WA
Deltona	FL	Lee's Summit	MO	Tacoma	WA
Hollywood	FL	Mexico	MO	Vancouver	WA
Miami Springs	FL	Asheville	NC	Brookfield	WI
New Smyrna Beach	FL	Cary	NC	Franklin	WI
North Miami Beach	FL	Charlotte	NC	Green Bay	WI
Orlando	FL	Concord	NC	Kaukauna	WI
Palm Bay	FL	Hickory	NC	La Crosse	WI
Pensacola	FL	Jacksonville	NC	Madison	WI
Pinellas Park	FL	Winston-Salem	NC	Two Rivers	WI
St. Petersburg	FL	Bismarck	ND	Laramie	WY

Appendix E
Economic Development and
Technology Economy Survey

The objective of the Economic Development and Technology Economy Survey is to gauge the role of telecommunications in the economic development efforts of cities. Without your help, we cannot present a complete picture.

For the purpose of this survey, **telecommunications** includes provision of telecommunications services (voice, video, or data) by an entity authorized to provide telecommunications services to the general public and Internet service providers. **Telecommunications/technology infrastructure** includes conduits, cables, poles, wires, lines, towers, easements, property, and routes used, operated, owned, or controlled by any entity providing telecommunications services.

Unless otherwise indicated, please *check the box* or *circle the option* by the appropriate response.

Name of your city or town_____ State _____

Please provide the contact information for the individual who completed or who can answer questions about this questionnaire. (Please keep a copy of the completed survey for your files should we need to call.)

Name: _____ Title: _____

Address: _____

City: _____ State: _____ Zip: _____

Phone number: (_____) _____ E-Mail:_____

Economic Development Efforts

1. Approximately how many full-time employees in your city are directly focused on economic development and redevelopment, including within city government and in any external agency? (Check one)

    a. Fewer than 3 employees   59%
    b. 3–5 employees   20%
    c. More than 5 employees   21%

2. What percentage of economic development staff time is devoted to the following activities?

    a. Business attraction   37% (mean)
    b. Business retention   33% (mean)
    c. Other development   37% (mean)

3. How much did your local government budget for economic development activities for:

    a. FY2000 $1,417,000 (mean)
    b. FY2001 $1,411,000 (mean)
    c. FY2002 (Budgeted) $1,491,000 (mean)
    d. List the top three funded activities in FY2001
        (i) 1. Advertising/Trade show/Exhibit
            2. Personnel/Consulting
            3. Infrastructure/Public works

4. Have your economic development efforts increased job growth?
        Yes   79%
        No   5%
        Don't know   16%

    a. If yes, how many jobs were created?   920 (mean)
    b. How much employment growth was this (percent of total growth)?
       32% (mean)
    c. What types of jobs were created? (Check all that apply)
       (% selecting option)
       (i)   Full-time   99%
       (ii)   Part-time   65%
       (iii) High-wage   82%
       (iv)   Low-wage   83%
       (v)   High-skilled   78%
       (vi)   Low-skilled   83%

The Role of Technology Economy and Telecommunications in Local Economies

5. Where does the technology economy/telecommunications fit into your economy? (*Rank* the following responses, with the best fit being 1)
    (% ranking "best fit")

    As an economic sector   20%
    As an undeveloped factor   36%
    As a critical infrastructure that facilitates other sectors 68%
    Other   19%

6. How does telecommunications availability/capacity contribute to your locale's future economic viability? (Check one)

   a. Telecommunications is an essential component.   57%
   b. Telecommunications is a major component.   23%
   c. Telecommunications is a small component.   16%
   d. Telecommunications is not relevant.   2%
   e. Don't know   2%

7. How important are advanced telecommunications services to the daily operations of businesses in your jurisdiction? (Check one)

   a. Not important   2%
   b. Relatively unimportant   9%
   c. Relatively important   42%
   d. Very important   47%

8. Does your local government have an economic development plan that addresses telecommunications infrastructure?

   a. No   77%
      (i)   Do you intend to develop such a plan with the next two years?
            Yes 47%   No 12%   Don't know 41%
   b. Yes 21%
      (i)   If yes, what year was it developed? *(most often cited responses)*
            2001 (28%), 1998 (17%), 2000 (15%)
      (ii) What year was it most recently updated? *(most often cited responses)*
            2002 (49%), 2001 (48%)
   c. Don't know 2%

9. Does your local government use the jurisdiction's telecommunications/technology infrastructure as a tool or asset in promoting economic development?

   Yes   63%
   No   32%
   Don't know   5%

   a. If yes, do you use it mainly to: (Check all that apply) *(% selecting option)*
      (i)   Attract specific businesses   79%
      (ii) Increase jobs   56%
      (iii) Reduce poverty   15%
      (iv) General redevelopment   52%

10. Do your local government's strategies or plans include any of the following: (Check all that apply) *(% selecting option)*

    a. Deployment of fiber-optic cable/network   62%
    b. Technology zones   19%
    c. Telecommunications/Technology incubators   29%
    d. Smart buildings (e.g., equipped with advanced
       telecommunications services and technologies)   32%
    e. Regulatory flexibility to attract telecommunications providers   18%
    f. Tax incentives for telecommunications   18%
    g. Intelligent vehicle highway systems (e.g., electronic toll collectors)   11%
    h. Use the Internet or website to advertise and promote the locale   82%

11. What hurdles exist in preventing the use of telecommunications/technology as part of your local government's economic development strategy? (Check all that apply) *(% selecting option)*

    a. Federal/State regulatory control   20%
    b. Private sector ownership   35%
    c. Lack of local government support   15%
    d. Planning bodies that dictate permitting   5%
    e. Lack of funding   69%

Telecommunications/Technology Infrastructure Assessment

12. Is there a publicly funded Internet backbone (fiber-optic loop) in your state?
    Yes   38%
    No   24%
    Don't know   38%

    a. If yes, does your jurisdiction utilize this capacity (connection)?
    Yes   47%
    No   30%
    Don't know   23%

13. Estimate how far your jurisdiction is from a privately operated Internet backbone.
    9 miles (mean)

14. Does your local government own a telecommunications utility?
    Yes   6%
    No   88%
    Don't know   6%

15. Please indicate the availability and ownership of the following physical telecommunications/technology pathways in your jurisdiction. (Circle 1 for local government, 2 for telephone company, 3 for telecommunications provider, 4 for utility; circle all that apply) *(% selecting option)*

Infrastructure	Availability	Ownership			
		1	2	3	4
Fiber-optic	84%	16%	77%	50%	15%
Coaxial/HFC (cable)	71%	5%	23%	67%	16%
Wireless	72%	9%	36%	67%	7%
Microwave	42%	17%	30%	51%	12%
Satellite	48%	3%	10%	60%	7%

16. Does your local government control the rights-of-way in your jurisdiction?
    Yes   84%
    No   9%
    Don't know   7%

    a. If yes, do your franchise agreements with telecommunications providers include: (Check all that apply) *(% selecting option)*
    (i)   Franchise fee (e.g., percentage of gross receipts)   87%
    (ii)   Additional conduit or fiber-optic cable for city use   42%

    (iii) Reduced price for telecommunications services   19%
    (iv) Access for public use (local government, schools, etc.) 64%
    (v)   Information on location and type of
          telecommunications infrastructure   35%
    (vi) Service to underserved areas   8%

17. Do you have an inventory of the telecommunications/technology infrastructure and its location in your jurisdiction?

Yes	25%
No	57%
Don't know	18%

a. If yes, please provide location(s). (Circle 1 for downtown/central business district, 2 for industrial/commercial, 3 for office parks, 4 for outlying areas; circle all that apply) *(% selecting option)*

	Location			
Infrastructure	1	2	3	4
Fiber-optic cable	69%	61%	51%	30%
Coaxial/HFC	51%	51%	41%	39%
Wireless (e.g., towers)	66%	74%	51%	51%
Microwave (e.g., transmitters)	26%	28%	13%	13%
Satellite (e.g., facilities)	20%	15%	15%	11%

18. Has your jurisdiction's telecommunications/technology infrastructure been improved in the past 6 years? (Please include both governmental and nongovernmental improvements.)

Yes	83%
No	4%
Don't know	13%

a. If yes, who was involved in the planning and deployment of telecommunications infrastructure? (Check all that apply) *(% selecting option)*

(i)	Local government	53%
(ii)	Both public and private	42%
(iii)	Public-private partnership	13%
(iv)	Other private business	17%
(v)	Libraries and museums	14%
(vi)	Private telecommunications provider(s)	87%
(vii)	Nonprofit organization	4%
(viii)	Neighborhood organizations	1%
(ix)	Schools	33%

b. Please indicate (1) what type of telecommunications/technology infrastructure was improved and (2) where it was improved. (Circle 1 for downtown/central business district, 2 for industrial/commercial, 3 for office parks, 4 for outlying areas; circle all that apply) *(% selecting option)*

Infrastructure	Location			
	1	2	3	4
Fiber-optic cable	36%	36%	26%	21%
Coaxial/HFC	22%	20%	16%	17%
Wireless (e.g. ,towers)	25%	26%	19%	21%
Microwave (e.g., transmitters)	6%	5%	3%	6%
Satellite (e.g., facilities)	4%	5%	3%	2%

c. What were the objectives of the improvements? (Check all that apply)
   (% selecting option)

(i)   Attract business/jobs   55%
(ii)   Attract technology economy businesses   45%
(iii) Diversify economic base of jurisdiction   35%
(iv)   Increase tax revenues   31%
(v)   Downtown revitalization   20%
(vi)   Telecommuting centers   13%
(vii) Redevelopment   21%
(viii) Telco hotels (e.g., buildings rented to
          telecommunications tenants to house network equipment)   9%
(ix)   Leverage existing telecommunications/technology infrastructure 37%
(x)   Utilization of other physical infrastructure
          (railway, highway, sewer, etc.)   22%
(xi)   Provide service to an underserved area   45%
(xii) Enhance regional backbone and distribution systems   56%
(xiii) Serve special needs like schools, government,
          or publicly owned utilities   46%

19. How does the telecommunications/technology infrastructure in your
      jurisdiction compare to neighboring jurisdictions?

   a.   It is *worse than* our neighboring jurisdictions.   11%
   b.   It is the *same as* our neighboring jurisdictions.   55%
   c.   It is *better than* our neighboring jurisdictions.   34%

20. With regard to telecommunications/technology infrastructure, how do you view
      your neighboring jurisdictions?

   a.   Competitors   22%
   b.   Reluctant collaborators   17%
   c.   Partners   54%
   d.   Other   7%

Local Economic Base

21. Which of the following best describes your local government's primary
      economic base (1) during the last five years and (2) which do you think
      it will be over the next five years? (Check only one in each column)
      (% selecting option)

	Last 5 Years	Next 5 Years
Agriculture (farming and supporting industries)	8.6%	6.5%
Manufacturing	24.8%	22.0%
Retail/Service	30.0%	31.2%
Institutional (military, government, nonprofit, etc.)	10.4%	10.2%
Residential community (retired or commuters)	7.0%	2.4%
Tourism/Hospitality	3.3%	4.2%
Warehousing/Distribution	5.7%	6.0%
Technology/Telecommunications	1.5%	7.8%
Other	2.0%	2.6%

Notes

Notes to Chapter 1

1. These numbers are for 1993 and 2000 employment in information technology–producing industries, defined in the U.S. Department of Commerce's *Digital Economy* report in appendix table 2.1 (U.S. Department of Commerce 2003).

2. A list of high-technology industries with greater-than-average science and technology occupations can be found in Hecker 2005. The reported employment for 1992 and 2002 use numbers from Table 1 but do not include federal government or forestry industries. Data for 2004 are from the Bureau of Labor Statistics' Occupational Employment and Wage Estimates for May 2004, ftp://ftp.bls.gov/pub/special.requests/oes/oesm04in4.zip. These 2004 data also do not include federal government or forestry industries.

3. The Bureau of Economic Analysis defines this set of industries as information-communications-technology-producing industries. It consists of one goods-producing industry—computer and electronic products in durable-goods manufacturing—and three services-producing industries—publishing industries (includes software) and information and data processing services in the information industry group and computer systems design and related services in the professional, scientific, and technical services industry group.

4. States with such legislative actions as of June 17, 2005, include: Colorado, Florida, Illinois, Indiana, Iowa, Louisiana, Michigan, Nebraska, Ohio, Oregon, Tennessee, Texas, Virginia, West Virginia (Baller 2005). Also a number of states have enacted legislative barriers before 2005: Arkansas, Florida, Missouri, Minnesota, Nebraska, Nevada, Pennsylvania, South Carolina, Tennessee, Texas, Utah, Virginia, Washington, and Wisconsin (American Public Power Association 2004).

5. For example, in 2005 several proposed bills in the U.S. Congress, if enacted, would preempt local and state authority to regulate and levy taxes and fees on local telecommunications activities. See www.baller.com/comm_broadband.html for updates on these bills.

6. For a review of economic development research using surveys, see Wolman and Spitzley's examination of economic development politics at the local level (Wolman and Spitzley 1996).

Notes to Chapter 2

1. Actually, industries that meet both innovation criteria—research and development and proportion of research and development scientists and engineers—are primary technology generators, while industries satisfying only one of the criteria are secondary technology generators. Because my research is concerned with the most innovated technology industries, I will not analyze secondary technology generator industries. Thus,

when technology generators are referred to in the text, they are primary technology generator industries.

2. ZIP Code Business Patterns data items are extracted from the Business Register, a file of all known single-establishment and multiestablishment companies maintained and updated by the Bureau of the Census. The annual Company Organization Survey provides individual establishment data for multiestablishment companies. Data for single-establishment companies are obtained from various Census Bureau programs, such as the Annual Survey of Manufactures and Current Business Surveys, as well as from administrative records of the Internal Revenue Service and the Social Security Administration (U.S. Census Bureau 2001b).

3. Each ZIP code is matched to the appropriate city using U.S. Postal Service data and geographical information systems software. Aggregation of the data for each ZIP code in the city allows for an analysis of city-level numbers. Each city has ZIP codes with assigned Postal Service names different from the actual city that contained it. Using ArcView Geographical Information Systems, each ZIP code is assigned to the city in which a majority of its geographical boundaries are contained. Some ZIP codes were associated with more than one city. If a ZIP code was located in both city A and city B and the majority of the ZIP code's geographical boundaries were in city A's boundary, the ZIP code data were aggregated for city A. In addition, ZIP codes changes were also accounted for and corrected.

Notes to Chapter 3

1. For more on the survey methodology, see Chapter 4.

2. The Business Register is a file of all known single-establishment and multi-establishment companies, obtained from various U.S. Bureau of the Census programs and surveys.

3. The census defines an establishment as "a single physical location at which business is conducted or where services or industrial operations are performed. It is not necessarily identical with a company or enterprise, which may consist of one establishment or more" (U.S. Census Bureau 1992).

4. The 2001 ZIP Code Business Patterns data follow the same structure as County Business Patterns and the Economic Census. Due to privacy concerns, some employment data are available only in ranges (e.g., range A: 0 to 19 employees, B: 20 to 99 employees, C: 100 to 249 employees, etc.) to avoid disclosing the identities of individual companies that might be the only employer for a particular NAICS in that ZIP code. I use the standard methodology to correct for this employment data suppression, which is using the midpoints for employment categories in the low to mid range and progressively lower coefficients for categories with higher ranges. For the highest category, establishments with over 1,000 employees, the estimate for employment is based on employment figures for average paid employee per establishment from the U.S. Census, 2001. See www.census.gov/epcd/susb/2001/US/US__.htm. Although not a sophisticated method, the expected effect should be even across cities, which is why this is a commonly used method (see Chapple et al. 2004).

5. The means of employment for both technology sectors are significantly different at that 4.77e-33 level of confidence.

6. The coefficient of variation is a measure that is scale-free and thus useful to the comparison of the two sectors. The coefficient of variation is the ratio of the standard deviation of percent technology employment to the mean of that same variable.

7. In July 2005, San Jose became the tenth largest city in the United States.

8. Recent analysis of only science and technology industries in terms of absolute

employment figures in 1997 ranked large metropolitan areas, like Los Angeles and Chicago, highly. However, this is due to the use of absolute employment, where large areas are likely to have more because of sheer size of the area, but in terms of a percentage of the overall economy, these economies are very diversified.

9. For technology employers, the quartiles represent the following percent employment: (1) less than or equal to 2.34 percent, (2) 2.35 to 4.05 percent, (3) 4.06 to 6.00 percent, and (4) 6.01 percent or greater. For technology generators, the quartiles represent the following percent employment: (1) less than or equal to 0.79 percent, (2) 0.80 to 2.17 percent, (3) 2.18 to 3.88 percent, and (4) 3.89 percent or greater.

10. See Appendix C for descriptive statistics.

11. The Pearson correlation statistics between each sector and total employment growth in a city reinforce this finding. City total employment growth is significantly related to city employment in technology employers (0.126 at the .05 significance level) but not to employment in technology generators (0.025).

12. Patent applications vary greatly by reason for applying and by value, whether economic or intrinsic.

13. The patents data are from the National Bureau of Economics Research patent citations data file. The file includes data on all utility patents applied for from 1963 to 1999. In addition, there is a patent inventors file that includes the patent identification number and address of the inventor, whether personal or business. Using the patent and inventors files, I matched cases by patent number to create the number of patents by city for each year. Since a number of patents are applied for but not granted, I use only the number of granted patents. However, the data are truncated in 1999, so the data only include patents that were granted up until 1999. The time between patent application and granting is variable, but only those granted quickly by 1999 are included in the summation of patents for the years 1991 to 1999. I chose the summation of granted patents over the growth of patents because an artifact of the truncated data would make it seem that as we approach 1999, the number of granted patents decreased. This is merely a function of the time period between application and granting. For further explanation, see Hall, Jaffe, and Trajtenberg (2001, 9).

14. There are two urban classifications. In general, an urban area consists of a large central place and adjacent densely settled census blocks that together have a total population of at least 2,500 for urban clusters, or at least 50,000 for urbanized areas. A rural area is any place that does not meet the other urban criteria. All classifications cut across other hierarchies and can be in metropolitan or nonmetropolitan areas.

15. The Office of Management and Budget (OMB) defines statistical areas. A metropolitan statistical area must have at least one urbanized area of 50,000 or more inhabitants. Each micropolitan statistical area must have at least one urban cluster of at least 10,000 but less than 50,000 population. A principal city, previously defined as a central city in the 1990 OMB definitions, is the largest city in the core-based statistical area, but other cities can be designated as principal cities if they meet population and employment criteria.

16. The bandwidth data were provided by Sean Gorman, who collected the data from telecommunications providers over a six-month period in late 2002 and early 2003 as part of his dissertation research at George Mason University (Gorman 2004). The data indicate the total bandwidth between the two central (principal) cities in a consolidated metropolitan statistical area.

17. The FCC data report the number of providers servicing high-speed lines for each ZIP code in the United States. Simple aggregation of providers for all ZIP codes in the city would inflate the statistic since a provider will more than likely service high-speed lines in more than one ZIP code in a city. Thus, this aggregated number is weighted by

the number of ZIP codes in the city and then standardized by population or square miles in the city's jurisdiction to produce a relative comparative statistic of average high-speed/DSL lines per 1,000 population or square mile in a city.

18. The data were collected on August 4, 2004, from SpectraSite Cell tower data, and give the location of a wireless antenna and its associated network communications equipment. Rooftop towers are on building rooftops reserved for placing wireless antennas, which are typically used in crowded metropolitan areas. In-building towers provide wireless coverage to tenants within the building, and network equipment is housed in the basements of these buildings. These are generally in large metropolitan areas and experience heavy traffic throughout the day. Broadcast towers send transmissions to two or more stations simultaneously over a communications network. See SpectraSite for more information, www.mysitelocator.com.

19. Of the fourteen cities, only eleven voluntarily pledged a financial backstop in order to secure the first municipal bond to begin construction. The backstop amounts represented a portion of total network build-out, prorated by city population. The total amount to construct the network in eleven cities is approximately $340 million. The network in remaining cities will not be built out until revenues are generated from the operating network in the first eleven cities. See UTOPIA Financing for more information, at www.utopianet.org/overview/financing.htm.

20. City total employment growth is not included in the regression models because the purpose of the analysis is to determine the nonemployment factors related to technology sector employment.

21. There is no evidence of serial correlation, based on Durbin Watson test statistics.

22. The error variance is proportional to patents per 1,000 population; the model is transformed by dividing the dependent and independent variables and constant by the square root of the patents variable. This transformation corrects the standard errors for the coefficients on the independent variables, making the error variance homoscedastic, but it does not change the coefficients themselves (Gujarati 1995, 338).

23. The rule of thumb is that if the condition index is between 10 and 30, there is moderate to strong multicollinearity. However, none of the condition indices for the models are greater than this threshold (Gujarati 1995, 338).

24. Patents and college graduates have a strongly positive and significant correlation (0.592).

25. Telecommunications strategy usage is also a dichotomous dummy variable. Adding its coefficient to the constant $(0.190 + [-4.845])$, the mean of technology employment in cities with strategies is -4.655, which although negative is greater than cities without strategies.

Notes to Chapter 4

1. Of the total number of municipalities (19,429), there were only 605, or 3.1%, with populations greater than 50,000 (U.S. Census Bureau 2002a).

2. A similar sampling methodology is employed as part of the National League of Cities annual survey of city finance officers, published in an annual report on city fiscal conditions (Pagano and Hoene 2004).

3. I used the National League of Cities membership database to compile city and local official information for the questionnaire mailings. The sample includes all cities over 50,000 in population, and a random sample of cities under 50,000. I received 264 valid responses, or a response rate of 27.6 percent. As with any methodology, it is important that the sample can be generalized to the total population. I used the Census of Governments report on local governments for 2002 to compare the responding local

governments to the entire U.S. population of local governments (U.S. Census Bureau 2002a). The responses underrepresented local governments under 10,000 in population, with only twelve in this category (4.54 percent). If these local governments were removed from the sample and compared to only U.S. local governments with populations greater than 10,000, the sample more accurately depicted the number of local governments by population categories. Even with the truncation, the sample has a greater representation of small cities than the Census of Governments or the Census of the Population, which only report data for cities greater than 25,000 in population. To ensure a more accurate and complete comparison, I weighted the responses for the final sample of 252 local governments in accordance to the Census of Governments on four population categories. The resulting percentages of local governments follow the population range for each category: 10,000 to 49,999 (77.7 percent), 50,000 to 99,000 (13.5 percent), 100,000 to 249,999 (6.3 percent), and 250,000 and over (2.5 percent). Thus, the responses for all local governments are representative of all U.S. cities based on population. The margin of error for the survey is +/–5 percent, meaning that if similar surveys were conducted, 95 out of 100 times, the results would be within +/–5 percent of the results reported here. For individual questions, the total responses may be less than 252 cities, which increases the margin of error.

4. See Supreme Court's ruling regarding Missouri localities and telecommunications (*Nixon v. Missouri Municipal League* 2004) as well as proposed state legislative actions, as of June 17, 2005, in Colorado, Florida, Illinois, Indiana, Iowa, Louisiana, Michigan, Nebraska, Ohio, Oregon, Tennessee, Texas, Virginia, and West Virginia (Baller 2005), and enacted state legislative barriers before 2005 in Arkansas, Florida, Missouri, Minnesota, Nebraska, Nevada, Pennsylvania, South Carolina, Tennessee, Texas, Utah, Virginia, Washington, and Wisconsin (American Public Power Association 2004).

5. Passage of the Telecommunications Act of 1996 was chosen as the start date because the act was intended to spearhead greater competition in telecommunications by encouraging entry of new telecommunications providers into local markets and imposing mandatory requirements on incumbent carriers to facilitate competition (Telecommunications Act of 1996 1996). In addition, the late 1990s was a period in which there was considerable growth of fiber-optic and other infrastructure deployment. For example, fiber-optic deployment increased from 7.6 million miles in 1997 to 19.6 million miles in 2000, according to Telecommunications Industry Association reports (Telecommunications Industry Association 2002).

Note to Chapter 5

1. The partnership consisted of NewVa Corridor Technology Council (NCTC), Downtown Roanoke Inc., the City of Roanoke, the Roanoke Higher Education Center, and Cisco Systems.

Bibliography

Ahmed, Rashid. 2005. Interview by author. Senior Project Coordinator, Portland Development Commission, March 28.

"All Things Considered." 2005. "Boston Urges Better Cell-Phone Service." Available from www.npr.org/templates/story/story.php?storyId=4756347. Accessed July 2005.

American Electronics Association. 1998. *Cyberstates: A State-by-State Overview of the High-Technology Industry*. Washington, DC: American Electronics Association.

American Public Power Association. 2004. "State Barriers to Community Broadband Services." December. Available from www.appanet.org/legislative/index.cfm?ItemNumber=9998. Accessed July 2005.

Ames, S. 2001. "Cities: Bring Us Your Bandwidth." CNET News.com. Available from http://news.com.com/Cities+Bring+us+your+bandwidth/2100–1033_3–269084.html. Accessed July 2002.

Atkinson, Robert D., and Paul D. Gottlieb. 2001. *The Metropolitan New Economy Index*. Washington, DC: Progressive Policy Institute.

Audretsch, David B., and Maryann P. Feldman. 2000. "The Telecommunications Revolution and the Geography of Innovation." In *Cities in the Telecommunications Age: The Fracturing of Geographies*, ed. J.O. Wheeler, Y. Aoyama, and B. Warf. New York: Routledge.

Baller, James. 2005. "Proposed State Barriers to Public Entry." The Baller Herbst Law Group. Available from www.baller.com/pdfs/Baller_Proposed_State_Barriers.pdf. Accessed June 2005.

Barnes, William R., and Larry C. Ledebur. 1998. *The New Regional Economies*. Thousand Oaks, CA: Sage.

Beauregard, R.A. 1993. "Constituting Economic Development: A Theoretical Perspective." In *Theories of Local Economic Development*, ed. R.D. Bingham and R. Mier. Beverly Hills, CA: Sage.

Blakely, Edward J. 1994. *Planning Local Economic Development: Theory and Practice*. 2d ed. Thousand Oaks, CA: Sage.

Bleha, Thomas. 2005. "Down to the Wire." *Foreign Affairs* 84 (3): 111–125.

Bonnett, Thomas W. 2000. *Competing in the New Economy: Governance Strategies for the Digital Age*. Philadelphia: Xlibris.com.

Bradshaw, Ted K., and Edward J. Blakely. 1999. "What Are 'Third-Wave' State Economic Development Efforts? From Incentives to Industrial Policy." *Economic Development Quarterly* 13 (3): 229–244.

Bresnahan, Timothy, and Alfonso Gambardella, eds. 2004. *Building High-Tech Clusters: Silicon Valley and Beyond*. Cambridge: Cambridge University Press.

Bresnahan, Timothy, Alfonso Gamardella, and Annalee Saxenian. 2001. "'Old Economy' Inputs for 'New Economy' Outcomes: Cluster Formation in the New Silicon Valleys." *Industrial and Corporate Change* 10 (4): 835–860.

Brynjolfsson, Eric, and Brian Kahin, eds. 2000. *Understanding the Digital Economy: Data, Tools, and Research*. Cambridge, MA: MIT Press.

Cairncross, Frances. 1995. "The Death of Distance." *Economist* 336 (7934): 5–6.

Castells, Manuel. 1989. *The Informational City: Information Technology, Economic Restructuring, and the Urban-Regional Process*. Cambridge, MA: Basil Blackwell.

Center for an Urban Future. 2004. "New York's Broadband Gap." Available from www.nycfuture.org/images_pdfs/pdfs/telecom.final.pdf. Accessed November 2004.

Chapple, Karen, Ann Markusen, Greg Schrock, Daisaku Yamamoto, and Pingkang Yu. 2004. "Gauging Metropolitan 'High-Tech' and 'I-Tech' Activity." *Economic Development Quarterly* 18 (1): 10–29.

Charlotte Department of Transportation. 2005. Right-of-Way Encroachment Agreements. Available from www.charmeck.org/Departments/Transportation/About+Us/ROW+Encroachment+Agreements.htm. Accessed July 2005.

Chinitz, Benjamin, Thomas Horan, and Darrene Hackler. 1996. *Stalking the Invisible Revolution: The Impact of Information Technology on Human Settlement Patterns*. Boston: Lincoln Institute of Land Policy.

City of Lansing. 2001. City of Lansing e-conomic Development Plan Outline. Lansing, MI: Economic Development Corporation.

Clark, David, Sharon E. Gillett, William H. Lehr, Marvin Sirbu, and Jane Fountain. 2002. "Local Government Stimulation of Broadband: Effectiveness, e-government, and Economic Development." KSG Working Paper RWP 03-002, J.F.K. School of Government, Harvard University.

Clark, Kelly E., and Paul M.A. Baker. 2003. "Municipal Advanced Telecommunications Infrastructure Project (MuniTIP)." *OTP Policy Paper Series*. Atlanta: Georgia Centers for Advanced Telecommunications Technology Office of Technology Policy and Programs.

Clarke, Susan E., and Gary L. Gaile. 1998. *The Work of Cities*. Vol. 1, *Globalization and Community*, ed. D. Judd. Minneapolis: University of Minnesota Press.

Click! Network Tacoma Power. 2004. Project History, Tacoma Power website. Available from www.click-network.com/AboutUs/Project%20History/ProjectHistory.htm. Accessed August 2005.

Computer Systems Policy Project. 1998. *CSPP's Readiness Guide for Living in the Networked World*. Washington, DC: CSPP.

Cortright, Joseph, and Heike Mayer. 2001. *High Tech Specialization: A Comparison of High Technology Centers*. Washington, DC: Brookings Institution.

Council of Economic Advisors. 2001. *The Annual Report of the Council of Economic Advisors*. In *The Economics of the President*. Washington, DC: U.S. Government Printing Office.

Cronin, Francis J., Paul Hebert, and Elisabeth Colleran. 1992. "Linking Telecommunications and Economic Competitiveness." *Telephony*: 38–42.

Cronin, Francis J., E. Parker, Elizabeth Colleran, and M. Gold. 1993. "Telecommunications Infrastructure Investment and Economic Development." *Telecommunications Policy* 17 (6): 415–430.

Dedrick, Jason, Vijay Gurbaxani, and Kenneth L. Kraemer. 2003. "Information Technology and Economic Performance: A Critical Review of the Empirical Evidence." *ACM Computing Surveys* 35 (1): 1–28.

DeVol, Ross C. 1999. *America's High-Tech Economy: Growth, Development, and Risks for Metropolitan Areas.* Santa Monica, CA: Milken Institute.

Dholakia, R.R., and Bari Harlem. 1994. "Telecommunications and Economic Development Econometric Analysis of the U.S. Experience." *Telecommunications Policy* 18: 470–477.

Dreier, Peter, John Mollenkopf, and Todd Swanstrom. 2002. *Place Matters: Metropolitics for the Twenty-First Century.* Lawrence: University Press of Kansas.

Eisinger, P.K. 1988. *The Rise of the Entrepreneurial State: State and Local Economic Development Policy in the United States.* Madison: University of Wisconsin Press.

Elstrom, Peter, Paul M. Eng, Paul Judge, and Gary McWilliams. 1997. "It Must Be Something in the Water." *Business Week* 3541: 138–144.

Estes, Andrea. 2005. "Menino Maps Cellphone Gaps: Cruising to Learn If Dead Zones Tied to Minority Areas." *Boston Globe*, July 15, A1.

Federal Communications Commission. 2002. Local Telephone Competition and Broadband Reporting: ZIP Codes by Number of High-Speed Service Providers. Available from www.fcc.gov/Bureaus/Common_Carrier/Reports/FCC-State_Link/IAD/hzip0602.pdf. Accessed December 2003.

———. 2005. High-Speed Services for Internet Access: Status as of December 31, 2004. Available from www.fcc.gov/Bureaus/Common_Carrier/Reports/FCC-State_Link/IAD/hspd0705.pdf. Accessed August 2005.

Florida, Richard. 2002. *The Rise of the Creative Class.* New York: Basic Books.

———. 2005a. *Cities and the Creative Class.* New York: Routledge.

———. 2005b. *The Flight of the Creative Class: The New Global Competition for Talent.* New York: HarperBusiness.

———. 2005c. *The Rise of the Creative Class and Cities.* Washington, DC. Speech.

Forman, Chris, Avi Goldfarb, and Shane Greenstein. 2004. "City or Country: Where Do Businesses Use the Internet?" In *CSIP Notes.* San Francisco: Federal Reserve Bank of San Francisco.

Gibson, William. 1984. *Neuromancer.* New York: Ace.

Glaeser, Edward. 1998. "Are Cities Dying?" *Journal of Economic Perspectives* 12 (2): 139–160.

———. 2000. "The New Economics of Urban and Regional Growth." In *The Oxford Handbook of Economic Geography*, ed. G.L. Clark, M.S. Gertler, and M.P. Feldman. Oxford: Oxford University Press.

Glasmeier, Amy K. 1991. *The High-Tech Potential: Economic Development in Rural America.* New Brunswick, NJ: Center for Urban Policy Research.

Glasson, J. 1978. *An Introduction to Regional Planning.* 2d ed. London: Hutchinson.

Goldman, James E., and Phillip T. Rawles. 2003. *Applied Data Communications: A Business-Oriented Approach.* 4th ed. Hoboken, NJ: J. Wiley & Sons.

Gorman, Sean P. 2002. "Where Are the Web Factories? The Urban Bias of e-business Location." *Journal of Economic and Social Geography* 93 (5): 522–536.

———. 2004. "Networks, Complexity, and Security: The Role of Public Policy in Critical Infrastructure Protection, School of Public Policy." Ph.D. dissertation. Fairfax, VA: George Mason University.

Gorman, Sean P., and Edward J. Malecki. 2002. "Fixed and Fluid: Stability and Change in the Geography of the Internet." *Telecommunications Policy* 26: 389–413.

Graham, Stephen. 1999. "Global Grids of Glass: On Global Cities, Telecommunications, and Planetary Urban Networks." *Urban Studies* 36 (5–6): 929–949.

Grant, August E., and Lon Berquist. 2000. "Telecommunications Infrastructure and the City: Adapting to the Convergence of Technology and Policy." In *Cities in the Telecommunications Age: The Fracturing of Geographies*, ed. J.O. Wheeler, Y. Aoyama, and B. Warf. New York: Routledge.

Greenbaum, Robert T., and George E. Tita. 2004. "The Impact of Violence Surges on Neighborhood Business Activity." *Urban Studies* 41 (13): 2495–2514.

Gujarati, Damodar N. 1995. *Basic Econometrics*. 3d ed. New York: McGraw-Hill.

Hackler, Darrene. 2002. Economic Development and Technology Economy Survey.

———. 2003a. "High-Tech Growth and Telecommunications Infrastructure in Cities." *Urban Affairs Review* 39 (1): 59–86.

———. 2003b. "Invisible Infrastructure and the City: The Role of Telecommunications in Economic Development." *American Behavioral Scientist* 46 (8): 1034–1055.

———. 2004. "Information Technology Industry and Telecommunications: An Empirical Analysis of Cities in the Minneapolis–St. Paul and Phoenix Metropolitan Areas." *Journal of Urban Technology* 11 (3): 35–59.

Hadlock, Paul, Daniel Hecker, and Joseph Gannon. 1991. "High Technology Employment: Another View." *Monthly Labor Review* 114 (7): 26–30.

Hall, Bronwyn H., Adam B. Jaffe, and Manuel Trajtenberg. 2001. *The NBER Patent Citations Data File: Lessons, Insights, and Methodological Tools*. Cambridge, MA: National Bureau of Economics Research.

Hanna, Nagy. 1994. *Exploiting Information Technology for Development: A Case Study for India*. Washington, DC: World Bank.

Hecker, Daniel E. 2005. "High-Technology Employment: A NAICS-based Update." *Monthly Labor Review* 128 (7): 57–72.

Hilton, Margaret. 2001. "Information Technology Workers in the New Economy." *Monthly Labor Review* 124 (6): 41–45.

Horan, Thomas A. 2000. *Digital Places: Building Our City of Bits*. Washington, DC: Urban Land Institute.

Input. 2004a. "State and Local E-Government Spending to Double by 2008." Available from www.input.com/external/resources/about_news_detail.cfm?article_id=949. Accessed July 2005.

———. 2004b. "State and Local Market Analysis: E-Government MarketView." Available from www.input.com/external/emails/download/INPUT_SL_EGOV_MV_Summary.pdf. Accessed July 2005.

———. 2005. "Federal E-Government Spending to Increase Nearly 40 Percent over Next Five Years." Available from www.input.com/external/resources/about_news_detail.cfm?article_id=997. Accessed July 2005.

International Telecommunication Union. 2003. "Top Economies by Broadband Penetration." Available from www.itu.int/ITU-D/ict/statistics/at_glance/top20_broad_2003.html. Accessed July 2005.

———. 2005a. "ITU's New Broadband Statistics for 1 January 2005." Available from www.itu.int/osg/spu/newslog/ITUs+New+Broadband+Statistics+For+1+January+2005.aspx. Accessed July 2005.

————. 2005b. *World Telecommunication Indicators Handbook.* 8th ed. Geneva: International Telecommunication Union.

Jacobs, Jane. 1969. *The Economy of Cities.* New York: Random House.

Jorgenson, Dale W. 2001. "Information Technology and the U.S. Economy." *American Economic Review* 91 (1): 1–32.

Jorgenson, Dale W., Mun S. Ho, and Kevin J. Stiroh. 2002. "Projecting Productivity Growth: Lessons from the U.S. Growth Resurgence." *Federal Reserve Bank of Atlanta Economic Review* 87 (3): 1–13.

Jorgenson, Dale W., and Kevin J. Stiroh. 2000. "Raising the Speed Limit: U.S. Economic Growth in the Information Age." *Brookings Papers on Economic Activity* 1 (1): 125–211.

Kelly, Kevin. 1998. *New Rules for the New Economy: 10 Radical Strategies for a Connected World.* New York: Viking.

Kling, Rob, and Roberta Lamb. 2000. "IT and Organizational Change in Digital Economies: A Sociotechnical Approach. In *Understanding the Digital Economy: Data, Tools, and Research,* ed. E. Brynjolfsson and B. Kahin. Cambridge, MA: MIT Press.

Knox, P.L. 1996. "Globalization and Urban Change." *Urban Geography* 17: 115–117.

Kotkin, Joel. 2000. *The New Geography: How the Digital Revolution Is Reshaping the American Landscape.* New York: Random House.

Lansing Economic Development Corporation. 2003. "The City of Lansing IT Initiative: Continuing to Bring Technology to Everyone." Available from mayor.cityoflansingmi.com/it_initiative/Chapter2.pdf. Accessed July 2005.

Lee, Heejin, Robert M. O'Keefe, and Kyounglim Yun. 2003. "The Growth of Broadband and Electronic Commerce in South Korea: Contributing Factors." *The Information Society* 19: 81–93.

Leibowitz, Jay. 2005. "Municipal Broadband: Should Cities Have a Voice?" National Association of Telecommunications Officers and Advisors meeting, Washington, DC, September 22. Available from www.ftc.gov/speeches/leibowitz/050922municipalbroadband.pdf. Accessed August 2005.

Lucas, Robert E., Jr. 1988. "On the Mechanics of Economic Development." *Journal of Monetary Economics* 22: 3–42.

Luker, William, Jr., and Donald Lyons. 1997. "Employment Shifts in High-Technology Industries, 1988–96." *Monthly Labor Review* June: 12–25.

McDowell, Stephen D. 2000. "Globalization, Local Governance, and the U.S. Telecommunications Act of 1996." In *Cities in the Telecommunications Age: The Fracturing of Geographies,* ed. J.O. Wheeler, Y. Aoyama, and B. Warf. New York: Routledge.

Malecki, Edward J. 1991 (1997). *Technology and Economic Development: The Dynamics of Local, Regional, and National Change.* London: Longman Scientific and Technical. (Second edition published in 1997 by Addison Wesley Longman, Essex, U.K.)

Marcuse, Peter, and Ronald van Kempen. 2000. *Globalizing Cities: A New Spatial Order?* Oxford: Blackwell.

Markusen, Ann, Peter Hall, and Amy Glasmeier. 1986. *High Tech America: The What, How, Where, and Why of the Sunrise Industries.* Boston: Allen and Unwin.

Marshall, Alex. 2005. "Survivor's Guide." *Governing,* June: 60.

Mesa Electronic Streets Task Force. 2000. "Connecting Mesa: C-Net Subcommittee Phase I Report." Available from www.cityofmesa.org/econdev/pdf/connecting_mesa/mesa_estreets_report.pdf. Accessed July 2005.

Mesa E-Streets and Licensing Broadband Development Office. 2004a. E-Streets Infrastructure Opportunities Map. Available from www.cityofmesa.org/estreets/joint_trench/map01_14_04.asp. Accessed July 2005.

———. 2004b. "E-Streets Mission Statement." Available from www.cityofmesa.org/estreets/. Accessed July 2005.

Mitchell, William J. 1999. *E-topia: "Urban Life, Jim—But Not as We Know It."* Cambridge, MA: MIT Press.

———. 1996. *City of Bits: Space, Place, and the Infobahn.* Cambridge, MA: MIT Press.

Moss, Mitchell L. 1998. "Technology and Cities." *Cityscape: A Journal of Policy Development and Research* 3 (3): 107–127.

Moss, Mitchell L., and Anthony M. Townsend. 2000. The Internet Backbone and the American Metropolis. *The Information Society* 16:35–47.

National Science Foundation. Tables e-1 and e-6. Survey of Industrial Research and Development, 2000 [cited Tables e-1 and e-6]. Available from www.nsf.gov/sbe/srs/nsf03318/htmstart.htm. Accessed June 2004.

Nixon, Attorney General of Missouri, v. Missouri Municipal League. 2004. In 541 U.S. 125: U.S. Supreme Court.

Office of City Manager, and Office of Economic Development. 2003. *San Jose Economic Development Strategy.* San Jose, CA: City of San Jose.

Oliner, Stephen D., and Daniel E. Sichel. 2000. "The Resurgence of Growth in the Late 1990s: Is Information Technology the Story?" *Journal of Economic Perspectives* 14 (4): 3–22.

———. 2002. "Information Technology and Productivity: Where Are We Now and Where Are We Going?" *Federal Reserve Bank of Atlanta Economic Review* 87 (3): 15–44.

Oregon Telecommunications Coordinating Council. 2001. Oregon Laws Chapter 699. Available from www.ortcc.org. Accessed June 2005.

Pagano, Michael A., and Christopher W. Hoene. 2004. *City Fiscal Conditions in 2004.* Washington, DC: National League of Cities.

Paytas, Jerry, and Dan Berglund. 2004. *Technology Industries and Occupations for NAICS Industry Data.* Pittsburgh, PA: Carnegie Mellon University, Center for Economic Development.

Peterson, Paul. 1981. *City Limits.* Chicago: University of Chicago Press.

Pickvance, C.G. 1990. "Introduction: The Institutional Context of Local Economic Development: Central Controls, Spatial Policies and Local Economic Policies." In *Place, Policy and Politics*, ed. M. Harloe, C. Pickvance, and J. Urry. London: Unwin Hyman.

Pollard, Jane, and Michael Storper. 1996. "A Tale of Twelve Cities." *Economic Geography* 72 (1): 1–22.

Porter, Michael E. 1998. "Clusters and the New Economics of Competition." *Harvard Business Review* 76 (6): 77–90.

Portland Development Commission. 2002a. "Economic Development Strategy for the City of Portland." Portland, OR: Portland Development Commission.

———. 2002b. "Economic Development Strategy for the City of Portland: Appendix 2–7 A High-Technology." Portland, OR: Portland Development Commission.

————. 2005. Unwire Portland. Available from www.pdc.us/unwire/. Accessed July 2005.

Progressive Policy Institute. 2000. "State of the New Economy Index." Washington, DC: Progressive Policy Institute.

Randall, Robert W., Charles L. Jackson, and Hal J. Singer. 2003. *The Effects of Ubiquitous Broadband Adoption on Investment, Jobs and the U.S. Economy.* Washington, DC: New Millenium Research Council. Available from www.newmillenniumresearch.org/archive/bbstudyreport_091703.pdf. Accessed November 2004.

Regional Economic Development Team. 2003. Link Michigan Telecommunications Plan Summary. Lansing, MI: CRT.

Reich, Robert. 1991. *The Work of Nations: Preparing Ourselves for 21st Century Capitalism.* New York City: Knopf.

————. 2003. "High-Tech Jobs Are Going Abroad! But That's Okay." *Washington Post*, B3.

RHK. 2002. *Optical Insights.* South San Francisco: RHK.

Roanoke. 2001. "Vision 2001 2020: The City of Roanoke's Comprehensive Plan," 3.3 Economic Development. Available from www.roanokegov.com/WebMgmt/ywbase61b.nsf/CurrentBaseLink/E03AB26A54F9EA3C85256EF40063B740/$File/3.3%20Economic%20Development.pdf. Accessed July 2005.

Roanoke Economic Development. 2005. Technology Zone Program. Available from www.roanokegov.com/WebMgmt/ywbase61b.nsf/CurrentBaseLink/N25E9PGX802LBASEN. Accessed July 2005.

Romer, Paul M. 1986. "Increasing Returns and Long-Run Growth." *Journal of Political Economy* 94: 1002–1037.

Rondinelli, Dennis A. 2001. "Making Metropolitan Areas Competitive and Sustainable in the New Economy. *Journal of Urban Technology* 8 (1): 1–21.

St. Martin, Grege. 2005. "Menino: HUB (Boston) to be Wireless in 4 Years." *Metro News Boston.*

Salvesen, David, and Henry Renski. 2002. "The Importance of Quality of Life in the Location Decisions of New Economy Firms." In *Reviews of Economic Development Literature and Practice.* Washington, DC: Department of Commerce, Economic Development Administration.

Saxenian, Annalee. 1996. *Regional Advantage: Culture and Competition in Silicon Valley and Route 128.* Cambridge, MA: Harvard University Press.

Schmandt, J., F. Williams, and S. Strover, eds. 1990. *The New Urban Infrastructure: Cities and Telecommunications.* New York: Praeger.

Scott, Allen J. 1993. *Technopolis: High-Technology Industry in Regional Development in Southern California.* Berkeley: University of California Press.

Sommers, Paul, and Daniel Carlson. 2000. *Ten Steps to a High-Tech Future: The New Economy in Metropolitan Seattle.* Washington, DC: Center on Urban and Metropolitan Policy, The Brookings Institution.

SpectraSite. 2004. Site Locator 2004. Available from www.mysitelocator.com/. Accessed August 2004.

Stiroh, Kevin J. 2001a. *Information Technology and the U.S. Productivity Revival: What Does the Industry Data Say?* New York: Federal Reserve Bank of New York.

————. 2001b. "What Drives Productivity Growth?" *Economic Policy Review* 7 (1): 37–59.

Storper, Michael. 1995. "Competitiveness Policy Options: The Technology-Regions Connection. *Growth and Change* 26 (2): 285–308.

Strassner, Erich H., and Thomas F. Howells III. 2005. "Annual Industry Accounts: Advance Estimates for 2004." *Survey of Current Business* 85 (5): 7–19.

Tacoma Economic Development Department. 2001. *City of Tacoma Economic Development Plan.* Tacoma: City of Tacoma.

Tannenwald, Robert. 2004. *Are State and Local Revenue Systems Obsolete?* Washington, DC: National League of Cities.

Tapscott, Don. 1996. *The Digital Economy: Promise and Peril in the Age of Networked Intelligence.* New York: McGraw-Hill.

Telecommunications Act of 1996. Pub. LA. No. 104–104, 110 Stat. 56.

Telecommunications Industry Association. 2002. *Fiber Optic Network Capacity and Utilization: Part II.* Arlington, VA: Telecommunications Industry Association.

U.S. Census Bureau. 1992. Economic Census CD-ROMS. Volume 2B, *Manufacturing, Retail Trade, and Services.* Washington, DC: U.S. Government Printing Office.

———. 1997. Economic Census CD-ROMS. Volume 2B, *Manufacturing, Retail Trade, and Services.* Washington, DC: U.S. Government Printing Office.

———. 2000a. Census 2000, Summary File (SF4). Washington, DC: U.S. Department of Commerce, Bureau of the Census.

———. 2000b. County and City Data Book: 2000. Washington, DC: U.S. Government Printing Office.

———. 2000c. Lists of Urbanized Areas and Urban Clusters. Available from www.census.gov/geo/www/ua/uaucinfo.html#lists. Accessed December 2002.

———. 2001a County Business Patterns. Washington, DC: U.S. Government Printing Office.

———. 2001b. ZIP Code Business Patterns 2001. Washington, DC: U.S. Government Printing Office.

———. 2002a. Census of Governments. Vol. 4, no. 4, *Finances of Municipal and Township Governments.* Washington, DC: U.S. Government Printing Office.

———. 2002b. Census Regions and Divisions of the U.S. 2002. Available from www.census.gov/geo/www/us_regdiv.pdf. Accessed December 2004.

———. 2004. Metropolitan and Micropolitan Statistical Areas. Available from www.census.gov/population/www/estimates/metroarea.html. Accessed June 2004.

U.S. Congress, House of Representatives. 2005. *Preserving Innovation in Telecom Act of 2005.* 109th Congress, 1st session. H.R. 2726.

U.S. Congress, Senate. 2005a. *Broadband Investment and Consumer Choice Act.* 109th Congress, 1st session, S. 1504.

———. 2005b. *Community Broadband Act of 2005.* 109th Congress, 1st session. S. 1294.

———. 2003. U.S. Department of Commerce. Economic Statistics Administration. *Digital Economy 2003.* Washington, DC: U.S. Department of Commerce.

———. Office of Technology Assessment. 1995. *The Technological Reshaping of Metropolitan America.* Washington, DC: U.S. Government Printing Office.

U.S. Federal Bureau of Investigation, Uniform Crime Reporting Program. 1999. *Crime in the United States, Serious Crimes Known to Police.* Available from www.fbi.gov/ucr/Cius_99/99crime/99c2_01.pdf. Accessed May 2005.

U.S. Small Business Administration. 2004. *The Small Business Economy: A Report to the President.* Washington, DC: U.S. Government Printing Office.

Utah Telecommunications Open Infrastructure Agency. 2005. Community MetroNet FAQs 2005. Available from www.utopianet.org/metronet/faqs.htm. Accessed July 2005.

Vaida, Bara. 2005. "Clashing High-Tech Titans." *National Journal* 37 (39): 2918–2928.

Vaughan, Roger J. 1984. *The Wealth of States: Policies for a Dynamic Economy.* Washington, DC: The Council of State Planning Agencies.

Walcott, Susan M., and James O. Wheeler. 2001. "Atlanta in the Telecommunications Age: The Fiber-Optic Information Network." *Urban Geography* 22 (4): 316–339.

Wolman, Harold, and David Spitzley. 1996. "The Politics of Local Economic Development." *Economic Development Quarterly* 10 (2): 116–150.

Wong, Cecilia. 2002. "Developing Indicators to Inform Local Economic Development in England." *Urban Studies* 39 (10): 1833–1863.

www.InternetWorldStats.com. 2005. Internet Usage and World Population Statistics 2005. Available from www.internetworldstats.com/stats.htm. Accessed July 2005.

Yilmaz, Serdar, and Mustafa Dinc. 2002. "Telecommunications and Regional Development: Evidence from the U.S. States." *Economic Development Quarterly* 16 (3): 211–228.

Index

About the Author

Darrene L. Hackler is associate professor of government and politics in the Department of Public and International Affairs at George Mason University. Her current research focuses on the local political economy of cities in the technology economy, from telecommunications infrastructure to technology industry. She is also interested in information technology innovation in the non-profit sector. She has recently published articles in *Urban Affairs Review, Journal of Urban Affairs, Journal of Urban Technology, American Behavioral Scientist,* and *Annals of Cases on Information Technology.* She received her M.A. in public policy and Ph.D. in political science and economics from the Claremont Graduate University in Claremont, California.